WORKS BY W

Front Cover
MARY McEVOY
Interior: Girl Reading 1901

Back Cover
NATHALIE GONTCHAROVA
Gardening 1908

ISBN 1 85437 081 2
Published by order of the Trustees for the collection display 'Echo: Works by Women Artists 1850-1940'
23 August-29 September 1991

Prepared by Tate Gallery Liverpool, Albert Dock, Liverpool L3 4BB
Published by Tate Gallery Publications, Millbank, London SW1P 4RG
Edited by Judith Nesbitt
Designed by Jeremy Greenwood, Woodbridge
Printed in Great Britain by Printfine Limited, Liverpool

CONTENTS

Written by Maud Sulter

FINANCIAL SUPPORT FOR THE CAPITAL COSTS OF TATE GALLERY LIVERPOOL

The Trustees and Director are indebted to the Merseyside Development Corporation for their major contribution, and to the following for their generous financial support

Founding Benefactors
The Henry Moore Foundation
The Wolfson Foundation

Founding Patrons
The John S Cohen Foundation
The Esmee Fairbairn Charitable Trust
Granada Television & Granada Foundation
The Moores Family Charitable Foundation
The New Moorgate Trust Fund
Ocean Group Plc
(P H Holt Charitable Trust)
Plessey Major Systems, Liverpool
The Sainsbury Family Charitable Trust
The Bernard Sunley Charitable Foundation

Other Major Supporters
Arrowcroft Group Ltd
Barclays Bank Plc
The Baring Foundation
British Gas Plc
Deloitte Haskins & Sells
Higsons Brewery Plc
The John Lewis Partnership
The Liverpool Daily Post and Echo
The Manor Charitable Trust
The Pilgrim Trust
Pilkington Plc
The Eleanor Rathbone Charitable Trust
Royal Insurance UK & Royal Insurance Plc
Trustee Savings Bank Foundation
United Biscuits UK Ltd
Whitbread & Co Plc

Contributions have also been received from
The Beausire Trust
Blankstone Sington and Company
Charterhouse Tilney
Commercial Union Assurance Company
GMB
The Goldsmiths' Company
The Grocers' Company
Mrs Sue Hammerson
ICI
The Idlewild Trust
J P Jacobs
Kodak Ltd
The Members of Lloyds and Lloyds Brokers
Mr and Mrs Jack Lyons
Mason Owen and Partners
The Mercers' Company
Provincial Insurance
The Rogot Trust
J Rothschild Charitable Trust
Royal Bank of Scotland Plc
RTZ Chemicals Ltd
Schroder Charity Trust
John Swire and Sons Ltd
The Twenty Seven Foundation
Vernons Organisation Ltd
An Anonymous Donor

SPONSORS OF TATE GALLERY LIVERPOOL

The Trustees and Director of the Tate Gallery are indebted to the following for their generous support.

Abbey Well Natural Mineral Water
Abbeville Press
AIB Bank
Ashton-Tate UK Ltd
Australian Bicentennial Authority
Barclays Bank plc
The Baring Foundation
BASF
Beck's Bier
David and Ruth Behrend Trust
The Boston Consulting Group
Ivor Braka Ltd
British Alcan Aluminium plc
British Telecom
Bymail
Calouste Gulbenkian Foundation
Concord Lighting Ltd
Mr and Mrs Henry Cotton
The Cultural Relations Committee, Department of Foreign Affairs, Ireland
BMP DDB Needham
Goethe Institute, Manchester
Granada Business Services
Granada Television
Greenall Whitley plc
The Henry Moore Foundation
The Henry Moore Sculpture Trust
IBM United Kingdom Trust
ICI Chemicals and Polymers Ltd
The Laura Ashley Foundation
Merseyside Development Corporation
Merseyside Task Force
Mobil Oil Company Limited
Momart
Montblanc
P & P Micro Distributors Ltd
Parkman Consulting Engineers
Patrons of New Art, Friends of the Tate Gallery
Pentagram Design Ltd
Phaidon Press
J Ritblat Esq
Save and Prosper
Stanley Thomas Johnson Foundation
Tate Gallery Foundation
Tate Gallery Liverpool Supporters
Tate Gallery Publications
Tate Gallery Restaurant
Thames and Hudson Ltd
Unilever plc
VideoLogic Ltd
Volkswagen
Yale University Press

PREFACE

Artists are the most discriminating and demanding group within a gallery's public. They contribute a critical perspective to a collection which, as the *Artist's Eye* exhibitions at the National Gallery have shown, can be shared in a stimulating way with a wide audience. With this end in view, we have invited Maud Sulter to make a selection from the Tate collections, to form the first in an occasional series of exhibitions chosen by artists.

In selecting work by women artists produced between 1850 and 1940, Maud Sulter has brought a contemporary perspective to historic paintings from the Victorian and Edwardian eras, seeing them in a continuum with modernist works. In her essay, she reclaims for the present not just the body of work itself but the voice with which to speak about it. As an artist and poet, she has written a polemical commentary which is both allusive and metaphorical. She has augmented her thematic reading of the works with biographical information on the artists' lives and careers.

A collection is a history of sorts, partial and provisional. The Tate Gallery's collections of British and Modern art have been acquired for the nation over the last hundred years, and continue to grow. Maud Sulter has drawn attention to the absences as well as the presences within the collections. Her enterprise will generate further research and debate into the cultural values which underwrite these works, and the strategies behind them.

We would like to thank Maud Sulter for contributing such a fresh and challenging reading of the works selected. Her personal insight into these paintings, and her grouping of them, makes for a display which can be enjoyed on many levels. Scholars and art lovers will find familiar and less familiar paintings enriched with new meaning and value.

Nicholas Serota
Director, Tate Gallery

Lewis Biggs
Curator, Tate Gallery Liverpool

FOREWORD

Maud Sulter

It is always a delight to be invited to curate an exhibition. To be able to select works for display from a Collection as large and impressive as that of the Tate Gallery presents a wonderful challenge. My choice has been led by my passion for art. As a child wandering the corridors and galleries of the Kelvingrove Museum in Glasgow certain objects and pictures would draw me back to them time and again. An Asante stool of a Queen Mother, an Egyptian sarcophagus, Salvador Dali's 'Christ of St John The Cross', the Impressionists and Scottish colourists. Art can and does change lives.

Therefore when it came to selecting this exhibition I interrogated different possibilities and strategies. Through works by David Hockney, I could perhaps raise issues around class and sexuality. The Rossettis, Tissots and Sargents - those frocks! Think of the debates you could have around the politics of dress and the representation of women. Works by Landseer would provoke discussions about land ownership and notions of Scottish identity. Angelica Kaufmann's paintings would articulate discourse about women artists. By now you can tell that I had become quite breathless. So I put the decision on hold and began to reminisce.

Travelling in company and alone. Stumbling across Malevich in Amsterdam while on a trip looking for Blackwomen artists in Holland. I did of course find them. Basquiat in Edinburgh. A room full of Sekhmets in Rome on a trip with Claudette Johnson. *Blackwomens Creativity* in Northern Ireland revealed on a field trip with Ingrid Pollard. Black art in the Gambia. Wonderful discoveries made in the company of Lubaina Himid; Rosalba Carriera in Venice, Augusta Savage in the Schomberg, Egyptology in Vienna. Reading of Nan Hudson and Ethel Sands while on vacation in Dieppe, busily making 'Treatise on the Sublime' for our hostesses to exhibit in California. Memories flood in and the time has come to make a decision.

There is very little Black art in the Collection so I decided to further my continuing research into women artists in general. The main motivation of *Echo: Works by Women Artists 1850-1940* is to give to the many and varied audiences who visit Tate Gallery Liverpool the opportunity to see some wonderful works, several of which have seldom been on show since they came into the Collection.

I am sure that you will enjoy the exhibition and be delighted to draw upon the achievement that the works selected have now been published in colour, several works conserved, and an accompanying slide pack called *Women Picturing Women* produced by the Education departments.

I would like to take this opportunity to thank the many members of staff, both in Liverpool and in London, who have given so freely of their time and encouragement. No exercise on this scale is without its problems; however I have enjoyed myself immensely.

ECHO is dedicated to Nan Hudson (1869-1957) and Ethel Sands (1873-1962).

Maud Sulter held the Momart Fellowship at Tate Gallery Liverpool, 1990-91. She is an artist, writer and cultural historian. Her art is in the collections of the Victoria and Albert Museum, the Arts Council of Great Britain, the Scottish Arts Council and several private collections. She is undertaking doctoral research at the University of Leeds under the supervision of Professor Griselda Pollock. A current member of the Editorial Board of *Art History* journal, Maud Sulter has also researched and edited *Passion: Discourses on Blackwomens Creativity*, 1990.

ECHO: WORKS BY WOMEN ARTISTS 1850-1940

INTRODUCTION

SPRING DAY
Midday and Afternoon

Swirl of crowded streets. Shock and recoil of traffic. The stock still brick facade of an old church, against which the waves of people lurch and withdraw. Flare of sunshine down side-streets. Eddies of light in the windows of chemists' shops, with their blue, gold, purple jars, darting colours far into the crowd. Loud bangs and tremors, murmuring out of high windows, whirling of machine belts, blurring of horses and motors. A quick spin and shudder of brakes on an electric car, and the jar of a church bell knocking against the metal blue of the sky. I am a piece of the town, a bit of blown dust, thrust along with the crowd. Proud to feel the pavement under me, reeling with feet. Feet tripping, skipping, lagging, dragging, plodding doggedly, or springing up and advancing on firm elastic insteps. A boy selling papers, I smell them clean and new from the press. They are fresh like the air, and pungent as tulips and narcissus.

The blue sky pales to lemon, and great tongues of gold blind the shop windows putting out their contents in a flood of flame.

Amy Lowell, *Spring Day,* published in *Some Imagist Poets,* 1916[1]

In *Midday and Afternoon* Amy Lowell articulates a particularly feminist response to the modern city. Her perception of the light, the sounds, the experience of the city is centered on her response to feeling part of the whole, 'I am a piece of the town, a bit of blown dust, thrust along with the crowd'. Unlike the masculine *flâneur,* she delights in being part of the collective whole. Her understanding of 'the crowd' is not tainted by the bourgeois preoccupations of nineteenth century theorists such as Le Bon. She does not fear women being let loose in the city. Let loose to create their own states of being less trapped by the stagnant morality of the 1800s. The twentieth century brought to the city a new wave of women *en masse*, as consumers and shopgirls, as white collar and manual workers, as artists and writers.

The artists and writers whose works are explored in *Echo* inhabited both interior and exterior worlds. Their lives were negotiations between the public and the private spheres. The period in which these works were created, 1850-1940, was one of tremendous social and economic change in Europe and the Americas. The abolition of slavery and the following reconstruction. Feminism and campaigns for women's enfranchisement. In Britain in 1918 women over 30 got the vote, and in 1928 women were enfranchised on equal terms with men. The increasing use of photography as a means of documentation, categorisation and control. The struggle for freedom from European Imperialism in Africa, Asia and Australasia, continued.

The works in *Echo* may be consumed as delightful pictures which appeal to our senses on an aesthetic level. However there is further enjoyment to be derived from analysing them as works of their time. The relation between women and time is a fascinating area of contemporary study. In challenging the patriarchal nature of linear constructions of time throughout history, we can reveal numerous female rebellions against this practice, with the creation of other rhythms. As Frieda Johles Forman writes in her introduction to *Taking Our Time: Feminist Perspectives on Temporality:*

> Male dominion over time has been expressed in the mythology and iconography of Western civilisation with a virulence that has permeated all subsequent thinking on temporality. In ancient Greek myth, Cronus, son of mother earth and father heaven, who devours his own children, is identified with Chronos, the personification of time: thus our chronology. During the Medieval and Renaissance period, the allegorical linking of time and death becomes common iconography. The cannibalistic image of Father Time gives way in the sixteenth century to a more benign and paradoxical version: time is the ravager, as well as the revealer of truth, and that through a familial relation: 'Veritas filla temporis' (Truth the daughter of time).
>
> As late as in the nineteenth century, however, we still find the identification of time with death, Goya's painting of 'Cronus Devouring His Children', ranking as one of the most horrific works in art history.[2]

Ethel Walker's 'The Artist's Stepmother, Mrs Arthur Walker' c1899, is an important work in that it pictures one of the most contentious roles in the nuclear family - the stepmother. A character so often ascribed 'wicked' especially in children's literature. The role of the stepmother is tainted with the suggestion of being less than perfect. Not original. Unsatisfactory.

This anxiety therefore creates unresolvable tensions if the myth of the perfect mother is allowed to remain as central. However if the mythical 'perfect mother' is shifted and the marginal 'carer' brought back to the centre away from the periphery then, as in the Ethel Walker portrait, the stepmother can be reclaimed centre frame and allowed a space to be pictured as subject not object.

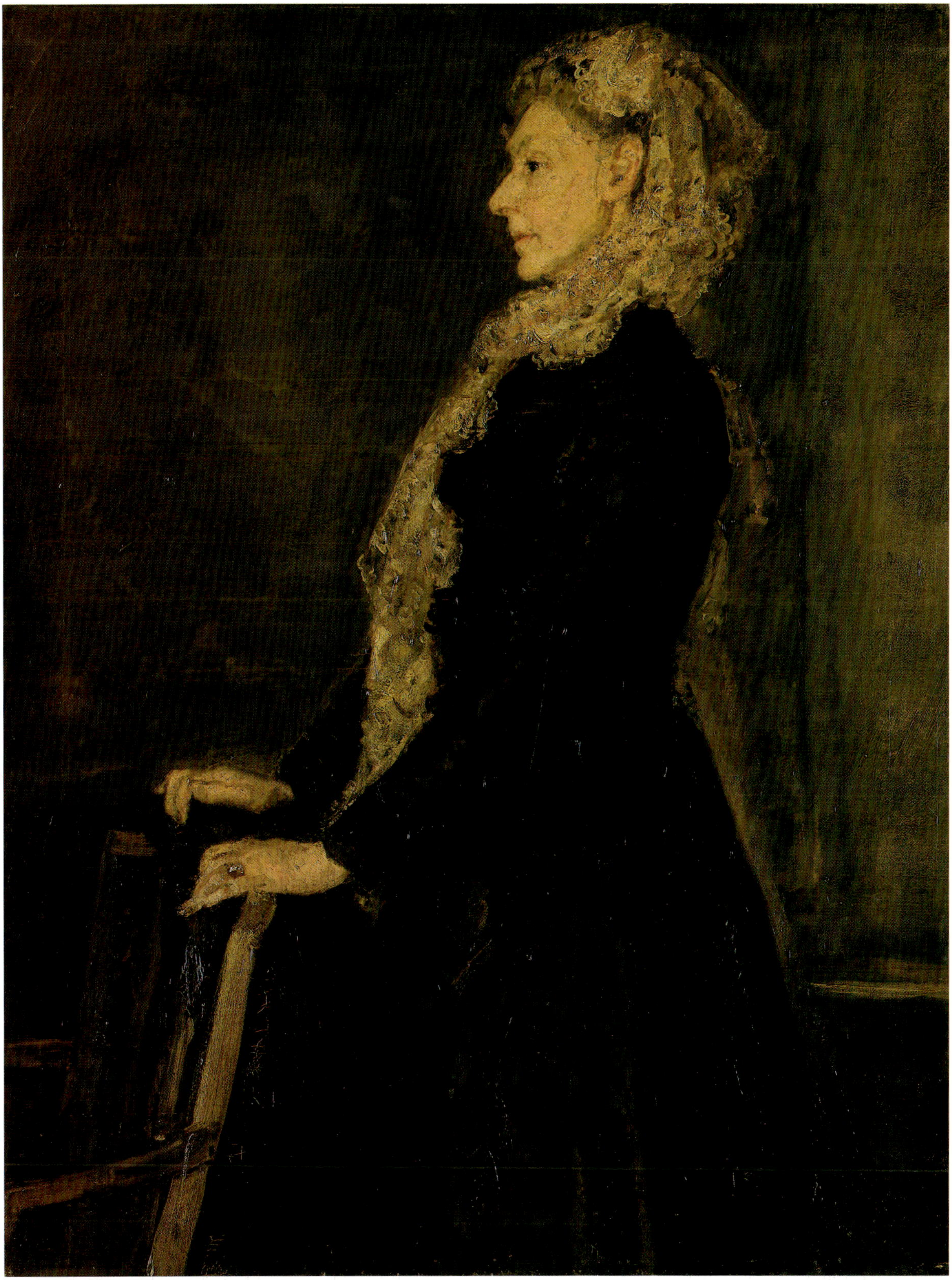

DAME ETHEL WALKER
The Artist's Stepmother, Mrs Arthur Walker c 1899 (not in exhibition)

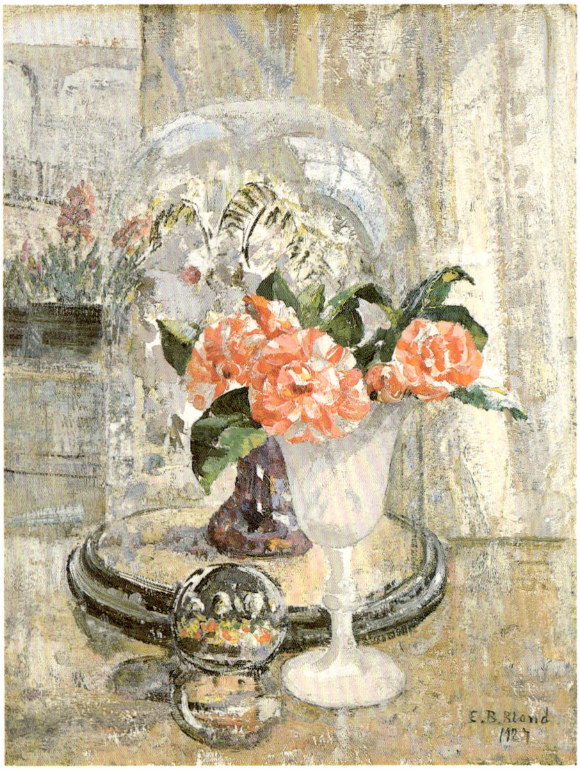

BEATRICE BLAND
Striped Camellias 1927 (not in exhibition)

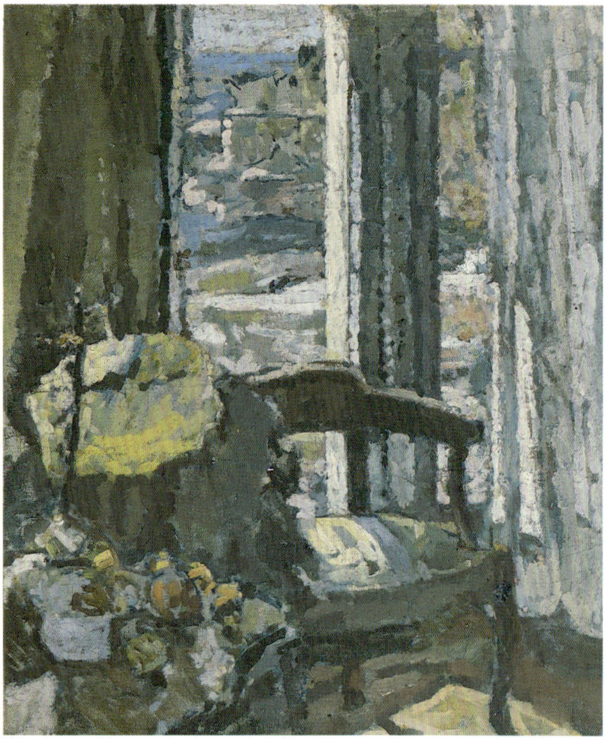

MADGE OLIVER
Interior, Pierrefroide c 1920–24 (not in exhibition)

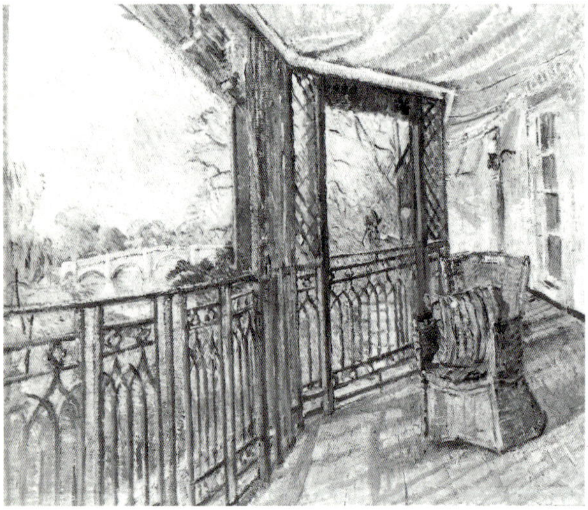

LOUISE PICKARD
The Green Balcony c 1927 (not in exhibition)

New critiques are appearing around the issue of still life and landscape painting. In her essay 'Looking into the Eyes of Flowers', curator and art historian Jill Morgan raises questions around female subjectivity in these traditional genres.[3]

Beatrice Bland was both landscape and flower painter. 'Striped Camellias' 1927 is fascinating because within its frame it articulates three states: containment, interior living and exterior continuity. Flowers, captured under a transparent bell jar, are set behind three striped camellias in an opaque white glass. Then we see through the open window, opening into the world, a windowbox of yet more flowers. These motifs and references are echoed in Madge Oliver's 'Interior: Pierrefroide' c 1920–24 and Louise Pickard's 'The Green Balcony' c 1927.

In Ethel Sands' 'The Chintz Couch' c 1910, pastels are used to create fierce parallel lines, the harsh white of the arum lilies standing tall and stately in a glass vase with the shaft of white light casting its rays down the wall and couch. The additional blue tones and touches of pink cannot

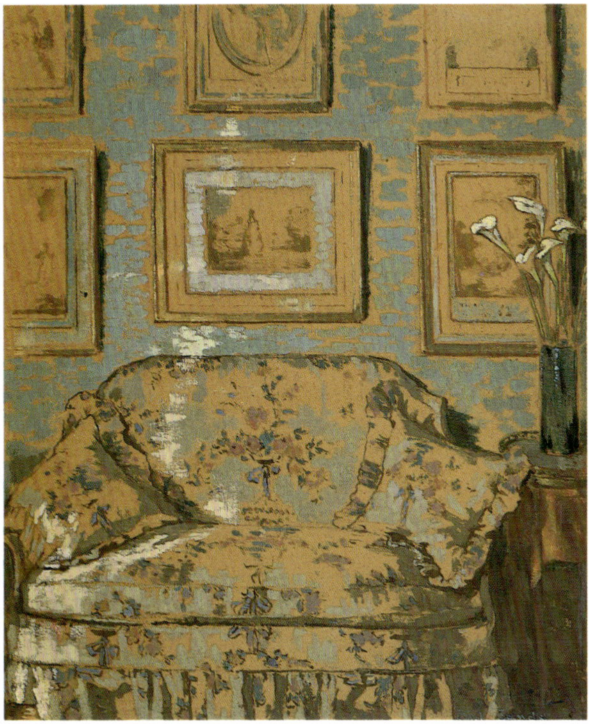

ETHEL SANDS
The Chintz Couch c 1910 (not in exhibition)

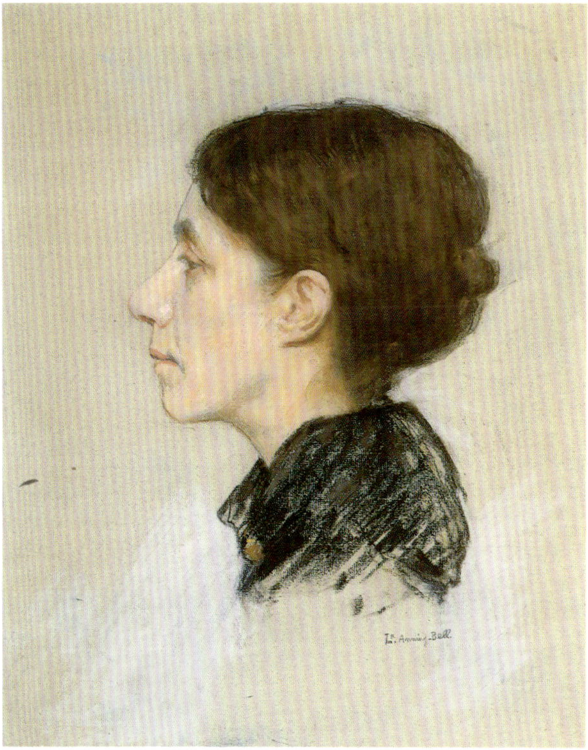

LAURA BELL
Miss Annie Horniman c 1910 (not in exhibition)

begin to compete and the viewer is struck both by the determined use of colour and the frustration that is aroused by this lack of compromise. The window through which the light enters is not pictured. As in Beatrice Bland's 'Striped Camellias' however, the suggestion of both outside and inside is inescapable. Pastels are again employed in Laura Anning-Bell's portrait of 'Miss Annie Horniman' c 1910, who was a pioneer of repertory theatre. She owned the Abbey Theatre in Dublin, 1904-10, the Midland Theatre in Manchester, 1907-08, and the Gaiety in London, 1908-21. This portrait was exhibited at the Paris Salon where the artist submitted work frequently between 1897 and 1911.

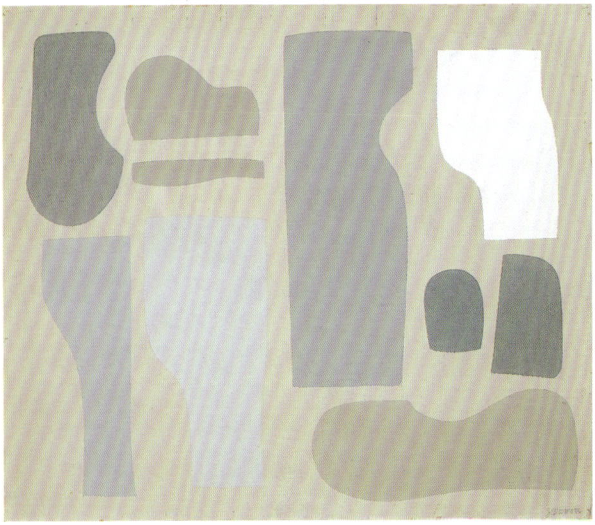

JESSICA DISMORR
Related Forms 1937 (not in exhibition)

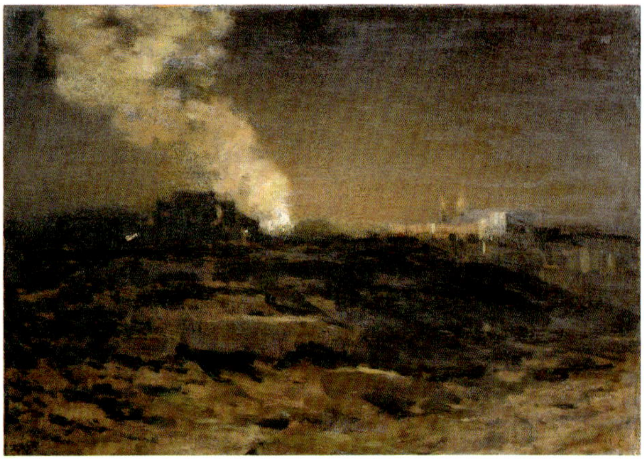

MARIE CAZIN
Evening c1884-88 (not in exhibition)

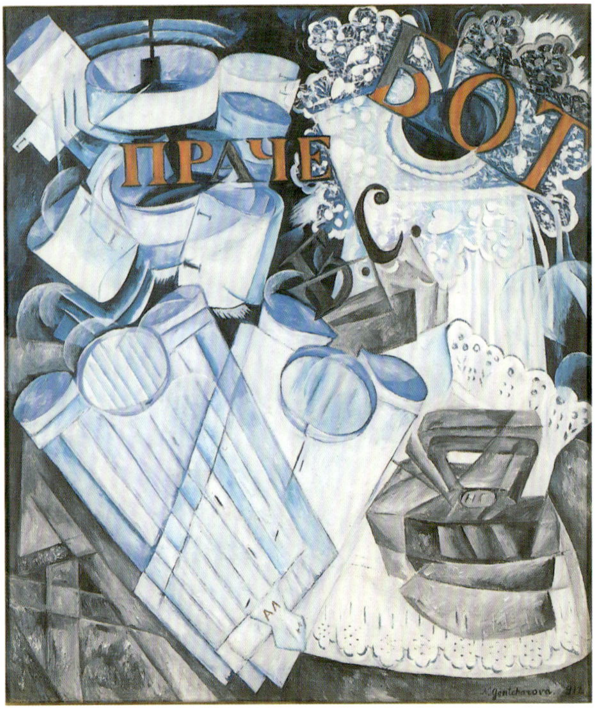

NATHALIE GONTCHAROVA
Linen 1913 (on display in *Dynamism*, ground floor gallery.)

Jessica Dismorr uses flat planes and tones to articulate 'Related Forms' 1937, whereas Marie Guillet (later Cazin), who was influenced by the teaching of Madame Peyrol-Bonheur, uses depth and sweeping brush strokes to evoke 'Evening'. This picture does not have a specified date and although the land represented may be Italian, this is not certain. There is uncertainty also as to the precise dating of Natalie Gontcharova's 'Linen'. However, as was previously noted, time can be translated through the potential for female rhythms which reflect temporal experience – rhythms which encompass multiple experiences; social factors, rememory, reproduction and creativity.

In 'Linen' we see pictured the domestic sphere. A heavy iron shifts provocatively in the lower right of the painting. Service garments, aprons, lace collars, all pristine and white, are arranged on the right. Here is women's attire placed in the sphere of women's work. To the left are men's shirts; both dress and day wear, and a multitude of collars and cuffs. Here is the dress code for the public sphere. Male space, male conventions. In this highly successful modernist work, the artist has refused the conventions of still life painting at the turn of the century and has focused instead on the creation of a feminist language in art. An articulation of women's lived experience made into art. Of course not all women have the opportunity to be full-time or 'professional' artists …

1939

...In her way, her strangeness, her naiveté, her craving for the other half of her equation was the consequence of an idle imagination. Had she paints, or clay, or knew the discipline of dance, or strings; had she anything to engage her tremendous curiosity and her gift for metaphor, she might have exchanged the restlessness and preoccupation with whim for an activity that provided her with all she yearned for. And like any artist with no art form, she became dangerous.

Toni Morrison, *Sula*, 1973[4]

Sula Peace, although a fictional character, became a rallying point for Blackwomen artists working in Britain in the 1980s. The novel seemed to strike a chord with many women working in diverse fields of creativity. The period in which it is set, 1919-1965, was a time of shifting locations prior to the revolutionary Black Consciousness period of the late 1960s and early 1970s, and of further migration South : North, Caribbean : Britain, Africa : Europe.

In resisting the urge to self-destruct, the artists who participated in the *Blackwomens Creativity Project* exhibition (People's Gallery, London 1985) and *The Thin Black Line*, (Institute of Contemporary Arts, London, 1985) had to draw on their own experiences, as our herstory is not easily accessed. Works by our Black foresisters do not seem to be hidden in the vaults of our national museums. Where their creativity does exist, it is mouldering away as the ethnographic exhibit.

So how, you may ask, are these observations relevant to a publication such as *Echo* which is written around an exhibition of works from the period 1850-1940? In acknowledging this absence we allow ourselves the opportunity to fill these gaps with our own scholarship, artworks, explorations. An absence can only be bridged by an active present. How we live now affects what those who shall follow us into the vaults of our national collections will discover in the future.

What works by Blackwomen will be there when they come to curate *Echo: Works by Women Artists 1940-2030?*

In my studio I have a collection of natural objects. The collection started when I became aware of the fact that more and more of the sculptures were resembling particular kinds of land and sea structures. These objects I have decided have their origins in a primal past. More specifically they are partly reminiscent of the very unlikely way these objects grow. Their relationship to the ground, or bulging out of a tree trunk continually arrests my imagination. They are ridiculous and wonderful at the same time.

I am trying to establish a sense of place both historically, culturally and psychologically. The word 'heritage' conveys a rich sense of tradition and security. But there is a sense in which I use sculptural language to make and explore boundaries in a contemporary context. The sculpture could be described as having a direct parallel with the very diverse ways in which human behaviour communicates, or remains alienated.

Veronica Ryan, in *The Thin Black Line,* 1985[5]

[The works illustrating this section were not available for display.]

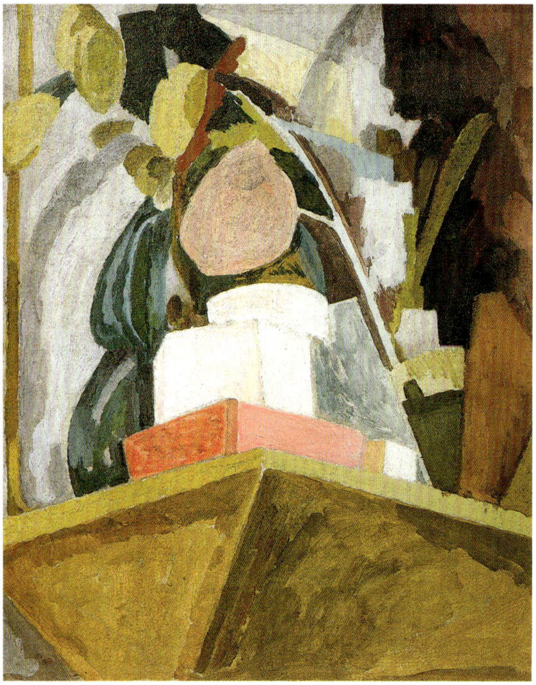

VANESSA BELL
Still Life on Corner of a Mantelpiece 1914

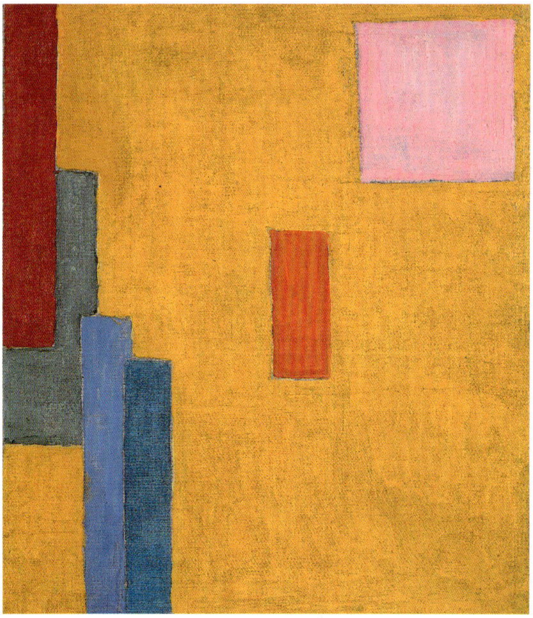

VANESSA BELL
Abstract Painting c1914

> Three years is a long time to leave a letter unanswered, and your letter has been lying without an answer even longer than that. I had hoped that it would answer itself, or that other people would answer it for me. But there it is with its question – How in your opinion are we to prevent war? – still unanswered.
>
> Virginia Woolf, *Three Guineas,* 1938[6]

Vanessa Bell painted 'Still Life on Corner of a Mantelpiece' 1914, and 'Abstract Painting' c1914, close to the outbreak of the Great War in Europe. Both demonstrate the conflict between order and fragmentation which was being played out in a particularly brutal way on the battlefield.

When my grandfather's brother, Jim, returned from the Front, it was in my Scots grandmother's kitchen that his feet were bathed for hours on end, still in their puttees until the caked mud freed itself from the fabric and would allow her to peel it away from the flesh. This took time and perseverence or his flesh would have come clean away like the spikes of a hedgehog baked in mud. And so the war once again entered Maud Elsie's territory. Her kitchen became a place of healing and refuge.

Allowing other people into one's domestic space gives them the opportunity to impose their opinion, as to how you live, onto their perception of how you are as a person, as an artist. An example of this prejudice is the fact that Vanessa Bell actively discouraged Roger Fry from inviting the painters Ethel Sands and Nan Hudson to be involved in the Omega Workshops, after having visited their home. In a letter to Roger Fry in the spring of 1912 she passed judgement on their creativity:

> It isn't what we want even for the minor art is it, I do think we shall have to be careful, especially in England where it seems one can never get away from this fatal prettiness. Can't we paint stuffs etc which won't be gay and pretty?[7]

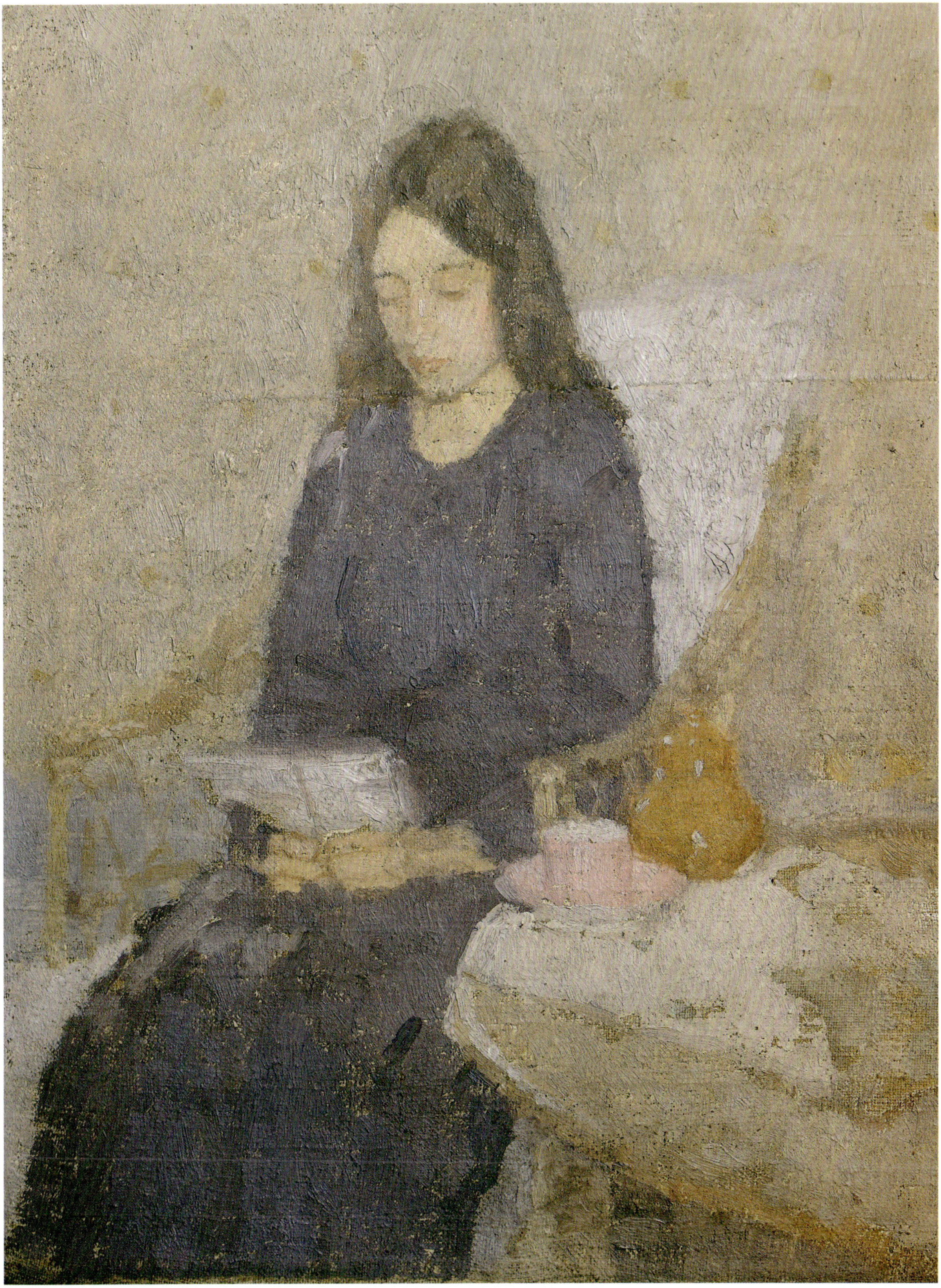

GWEN JOHN
The Convalescent 1918-19

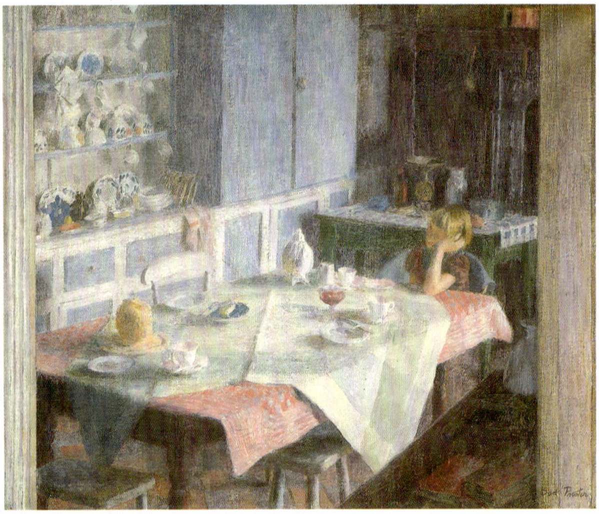

DOD PROCTOR
Kitchen at Myrtle Cottage c1930-35

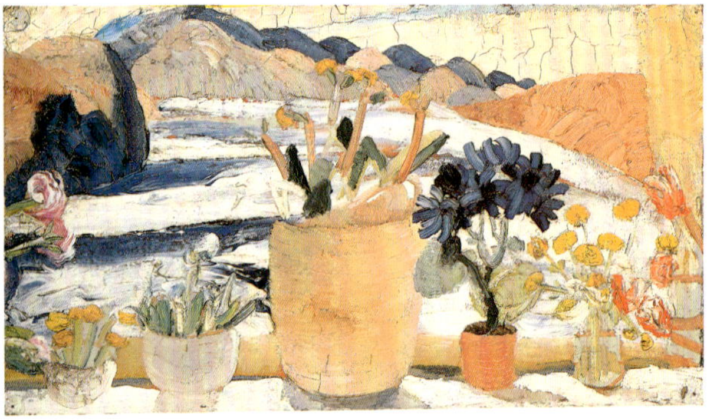

WINIFRED NICHOLSON
Window-Sill, Lugano 1923

As partner of Clive Bell she had been invited to spend a weekend at Nan and Ethel's country house in Oxfordshire. Frances Spalding in her book on Vanessa Bell notes that,

> Vanessa quickly perceived what immense care had gone into the choice of colours both in the house and garden: the grey walls offset with the white lawn curtains, the rich hues in the spotless chintzes and silks, the green and purple quill pens. Even the deep plum-coloured clothes worn by the two women, and decorated with orange, grey or yellow buttons, they seemed to have been chosen to match their surroundings ... she felt that the two friends lacked a creative freedom; they muffled or drove out feeling in pursuit of the refined.[8]

Confronted by such a wealthy and particularly woman-centered home, one may imagine that Vanessa Bell experienced some vestige of Victorian guilt about her more bohemian ménage. Bringing up two young boys, with so many people coming and going, with limited domestic help, and more than one painter in more than one house, did mean that such sophistication and freedom of expression was, for her, harder to attain.

Of course autonomous women's space is hard fought for and hard won. In 'Kitchen at Myrtle Cottage' c1930-35 by Dod Proctor, we see a girl sitting alone at a big kitchen table. She seems to be lonely. 'Where's mummy?' The kitchen is a feminised location in most societies. Whether it is the cook at the open fire of the compound or the Aga of the country-style kitchen, woman as nurturer is allowed access to the space which has been given over to the kitchen for the preparation of food as sustenance. Actually mummy is out in the orchard painting ...

Winifred Nicholson's 'Windowsill, Lake Lugano' 1923, uses the fact of a window frame to create a transition from inside to outside. The flowers in the room contrast with the landscape beyond. The interior contrasted with the exterior realm.

In Gwen John's 'A Lady Reading' 1909-11, we see the slight figure of a young woman (the artist?) sitting on the corner of a table with her right foot up on the cushion of a wicker chair and her right hand behind her back to aid her balance. In her left hand is the book she reads by the light of a window. The gay red and white gingham of the curtain is in contrast to the subdued mulberry of her simple blouse and long blue-black skirt. The curtain is pulled back slightly and held in place on the table by another book. Further back on the table lie some sheets of writing paper and a pencil. Perhaps the young woman keeps a diary. Or perhaps she writes letters. Perhaps she could answer the question asked of Virginia Woolf - How in your opinion are we to prevent war?

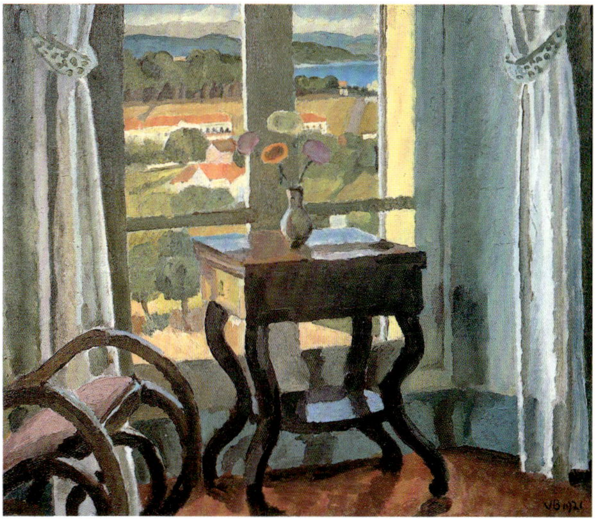

VANESSA BELL
Interior with a Table 1921

Saturday, 11 July, 1942

Dear Kitty,

... The 'Secret Annexe' is an ideal hiding-place. Although it leans to one side and is damp, you'd never find such a comfortable hiding-place anywhere in Amsterdam; no perhaps not even in the whole of Holland. Our little room looked very bare at first with nothing on the walls; but thanks to Daddy who had brought my film-star collection and picture postcards on beforehand, and with the aid of paste-pot and brush, I have transformed the wall into one gigantic picture.

The Diary of Anne Frank[9]

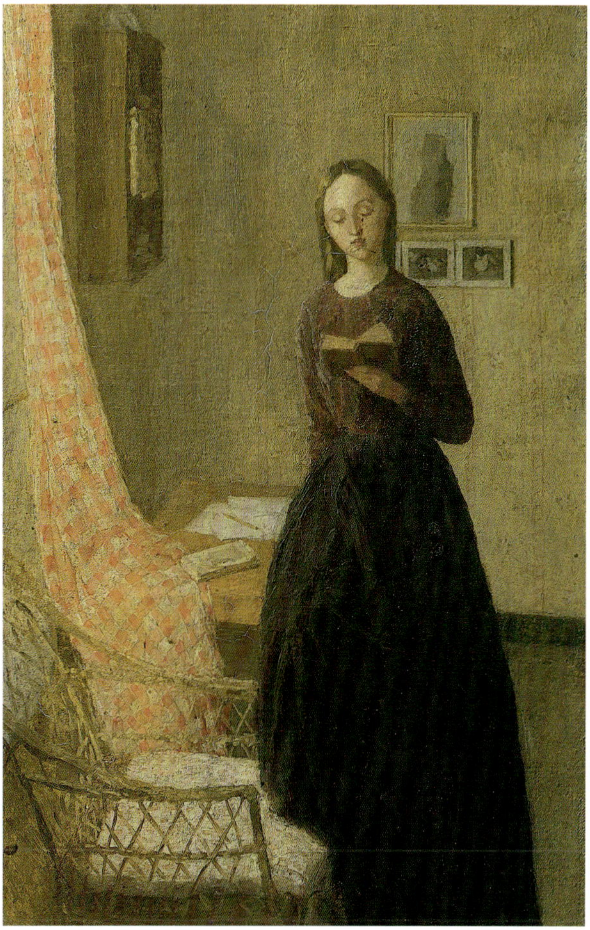

GWEN JOHN
A Lady Reading 1909-11

SCENE 1

It is going on nicely.

The place in which they stay is this one which surrounds. In the midst of suspicion that they will leave without them they may be an audience. As a reception of a difficulty they may manage to stammer. They will. Incline. To oblige. Only one. When they stare.

This is how millions mean.

This is a little a scene.

Just when they will go by adapting.

Nor may they be merrily there. To share.

Justly. In why.

It is a round movement this. Because. Declared.

For it. It is. A wonder. Because. They. Were. Spared.

Might it be agreeable if it were a mistake.

Gertrude Stein from *They Must. Be Wedded. To Their Wife*, 1931[10]

Gertrude Stein was one of the finest collectors of modernist works in the early part of the twentieth century. She lived for thirty-nine years with her partner Alice B Toklas in Paris. As Jewish Americans their choice of location offered them a freedom to live as they chose outwith the constraints of the *bourgeois* codes of middle class America. This motif of re-location to facilitate a chosen identity, and the conscious seeking out of communities with which to affiliate, symbolises, as for many of the artists in this exhibition, a desire to embrace issues of women's emancipation and an attempt to live by womanist codes and conventions.

Of course to live within society by codes other than those of the dominant hegemony, means a dual responsibility of creating new structures from fragments of the past which then inform the present. To be living in a territory, both physical and psychological, which is not yet firmly established, allows women a freedom to create their own visual and literary languages. By speaking in tongues, visions which have been suppressed or outlawed under patriarchy can be given voice. A new voice which attempts to articulate new ways of understanding women's place in contemporary society and new strategies to facilitate women's liberation.

One of the main strategies for creating these new discourses has been in the rereading and recoding of notions of femininity. And so we can observe in the following images of women painted by women, an active endeavour to articulate women's view of women's role within the societies in which the artists lived and worked.

In 'Loveday and Anne: Two Women with a Basket of Flowers' 1915, we see the seldom pictured everyday reality of women taking simple pleasure in each other's company. Frances Hodgkins contrasts a pout with a smile. Engagement contradicts evasive look. Stripes challenge floral chintz. Coiffure competes with millinery. The red, white and blue anemones in the basket on the table seem quite incidental to the scene. They are eclipsed by the picturing of two women who can agree to disagree and still remain friends.

The dynamic between artist and sitter is highly charged even when they are of equal status, gender, class and race. It is the artist's interpretation of the character of the sitter which comes down to us through history.

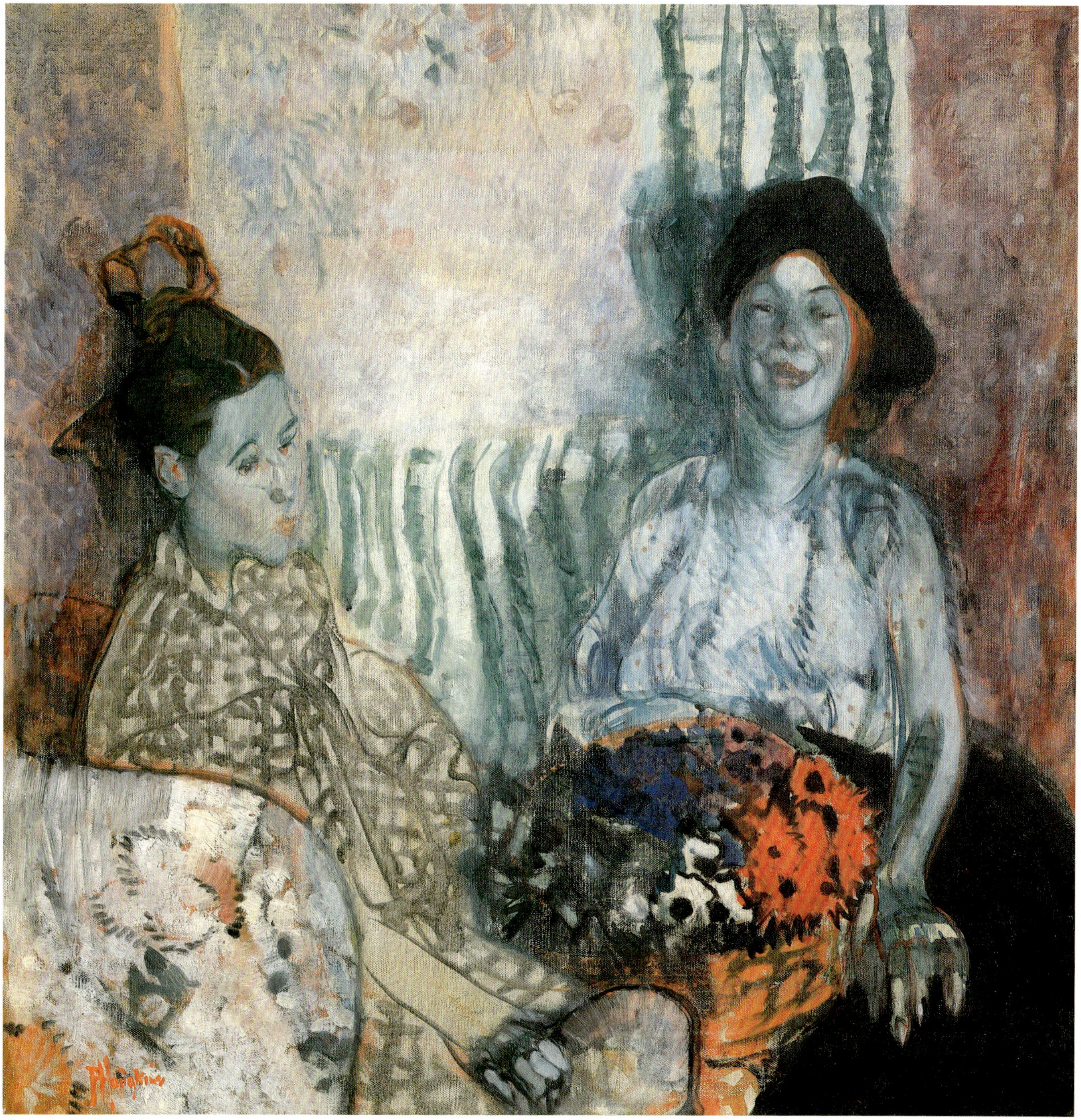

FRANCES HODGKINS
Loveday and Ann: Two Women with a Basket of Flowers 1915

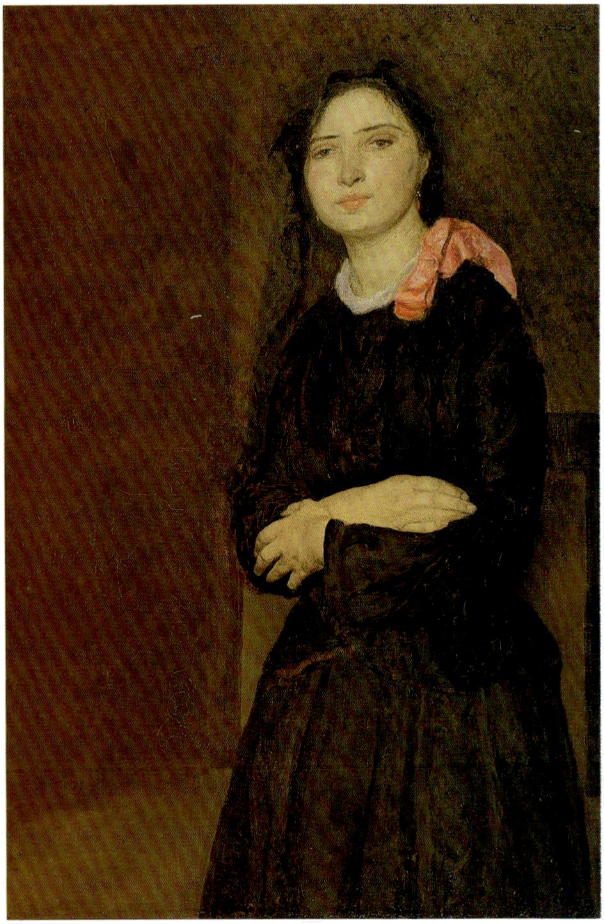

GWEN JOHN
Dorelia in a Black Dress c 1903-4

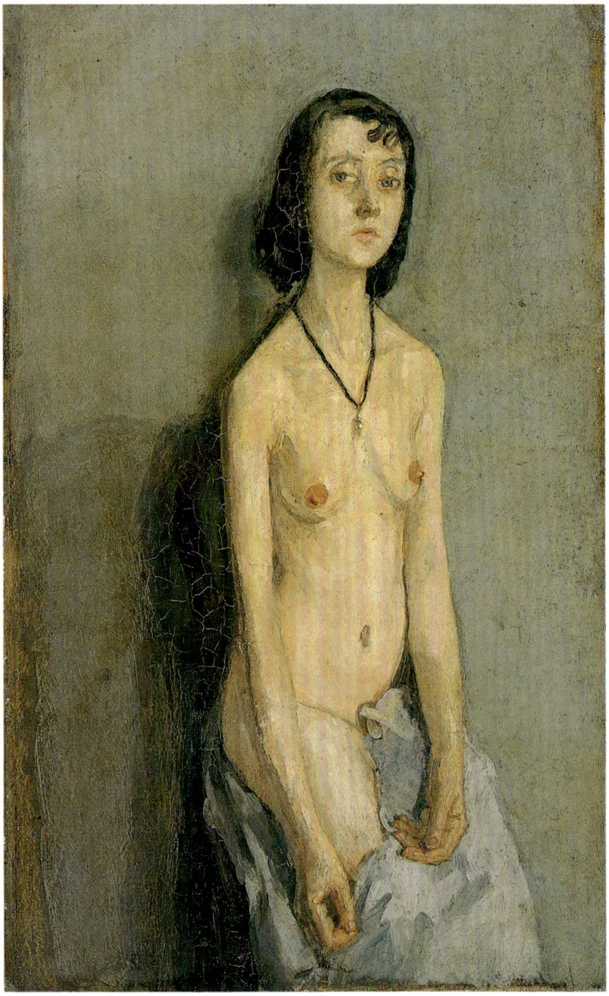

GWEN JOHN
Nude Girl 1909-10

Gwen John concentrated on painting and drawing women. Her studies made from models can be contrasted with the portraits of women with whom she had a more equal relationship. 'Dorelia in a Black Dress' c 1903-04, is a three-quarter length portrait of the friend with whom she had eloped to France in 1903. This fine portrait makes much play of the sitter's face and hands contrasted against the dark and heavy fabric of her dress. The gaze is direct and resolute. Like Ida Nettleship, also a friend and contemporary of Gwen's at the Slade, with whom Gwen went to Paris to study at the Académie Carmen, Dorelia MacNiell was lifelong partner to Gwen's brother Augustus. Such power dynamics are paramount in the political analysis of the picturing of women by women.

Fenella Lovell was the model for Gwen John's 'Nude Girl' c 1909-10. There is a parallel work entitled 'Girl with Bare Shoulders' c 1909-10, in the Museum of Modern Art, New York. In it the model is dressed. Her hair is neat, her facial expression severe. Yet in the Tate portrait the model is *déshabillé*, her hair has fallen forward onto her forehead, her gown is draped languidly from her crotch, and is only held in place by the chair on which she sits. Her hands still hold the same gesture but her face is now more vulnerable; her small bare breasts are pert. Around her neck hangs an adornment.

The sexual charge of these works is articulated

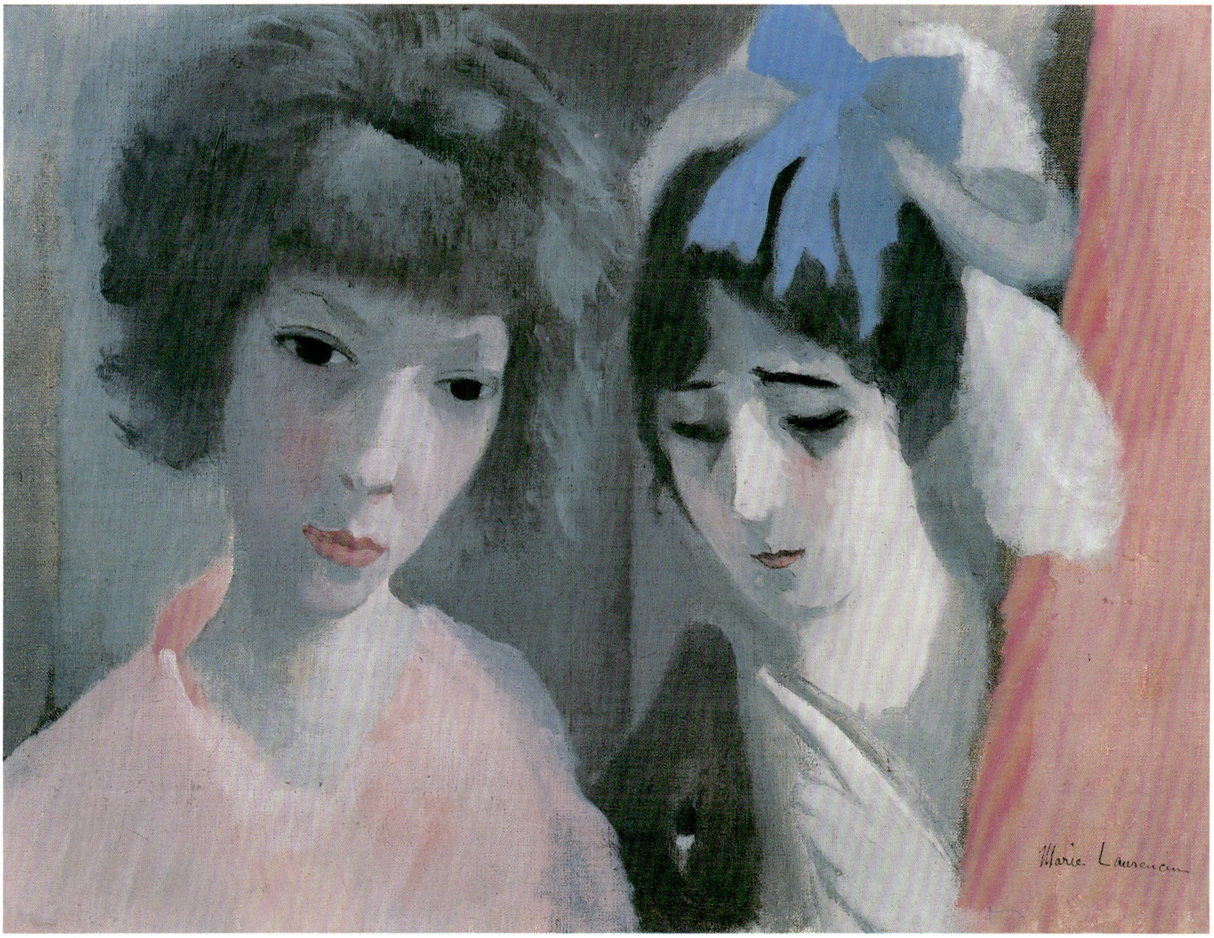

MARIE LAURENCIN
Portraits 1915

through the artist's resolute desire to question moral codes of respectability and the social *mores* which dictate that while 'woman' may be object of the male gaze there is still a prohibition on her being the subject of the female gaze. The work functions within a world where the dominant ideology is fixed on the issue of the representation of women as objects. As a work of art it is both aesthetically pleasing and is a good example of the complications women artists face when representing femininity.

'Portraits' 1915, by Marie Laurencin, depicts the artist with Cecilia de Madrazo, a young Spanish woman, in a beribboned hat, disciplining Marie's dog. It was painted in Madrid where the artist and her German husband were spending the duration of the war. The use of pastel tones and the elongation of the sitters' features is typical of Marie Laurencin's style and alludes to the artist's ethnicity.[11]

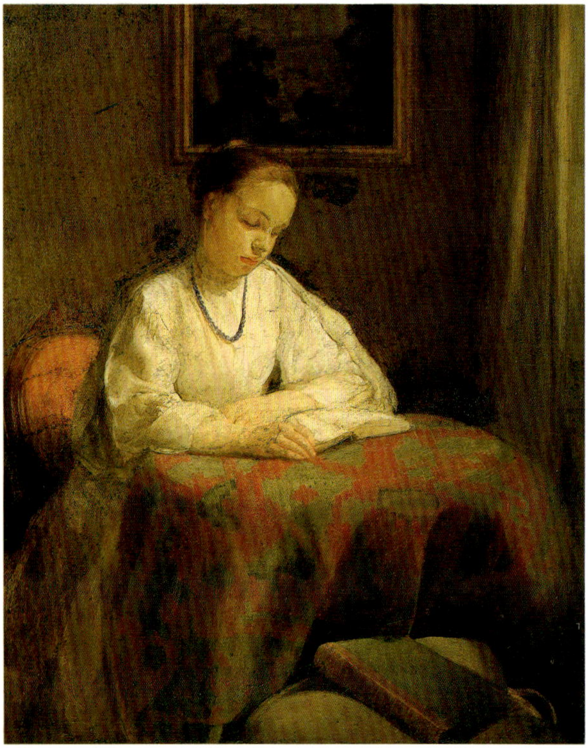

MARY McEVOY
Interior: Girl Reading 1901

It has been asserted that after marriage Mary McEvoy was content to prepare her husband's palette. This seems unlikely, given the obvious command and dedication to painting that is exhibited in 'Interior: Girl Reading' 1901. In the first moments of the twentieth century, for an artist such as Mary McEvoy to picture a woman at a table reading, signifies not only genteel acquiesence but also a quest for knowledge and new ideas. We know that the figure will continue to read whether we are there to witness or not. The composition is beautifully balanced between light : shade, absence : presence, interior : exterior. The painting of a painting within a painting, the representation of the woman, the recording of the Victorian interior, the quest for knowledge symbolised by the books, articulate both the concerns of the woman artist in Europe at the turn of the century and the techniques employed by them.

Frances Hodgkin's drawing, 'Seated Woman' c 1925-30, in pencil and black chalk, was made during the period that she spent working for Calico Printers in Manchester and travelling in the South of France and Spain. There are obvious Moorish influences in pattern and style. The features of the woman's face are stylised like an Akua Ma doll. Oval eyes, elongated nose and well delineated lips are precisely positioned on the flat plane of the face.

Mona Lisa was written by the African American author Angelina Weld Grimke. Angelina was born in Boston in 1880. She taught English in Washington DC. Her first play *Rachel* was performed in 1916. As a writer she was a regular contributor to magazines and anthologies of the Harlem Renaissance. A central concern of her writing was women's relationships with each other. After her father died in 1930 she gave up teaching, relocated to New York and took an apartment on West 151st Street in order to write. She died there in 1958.

A MONA LISA[12]

I

I should like to creep
Through the long brown grasses
That are your lashes;
I should like to poise
On the very brink
Of the leaf-brown pools
That are your shadowed eyes;
I should like to cleave
Without sound,
Their glimmering waters,
Their unrippled waters,
I should like to sink down
And down
And down...
And deeply drown.

II

Would I be more than a bubble breaking?
Or an ever-widening circle
Ceasing at the marge?
Would my white bones
Be the only white bones
Wavering back and forth, back and forth
In their depths?

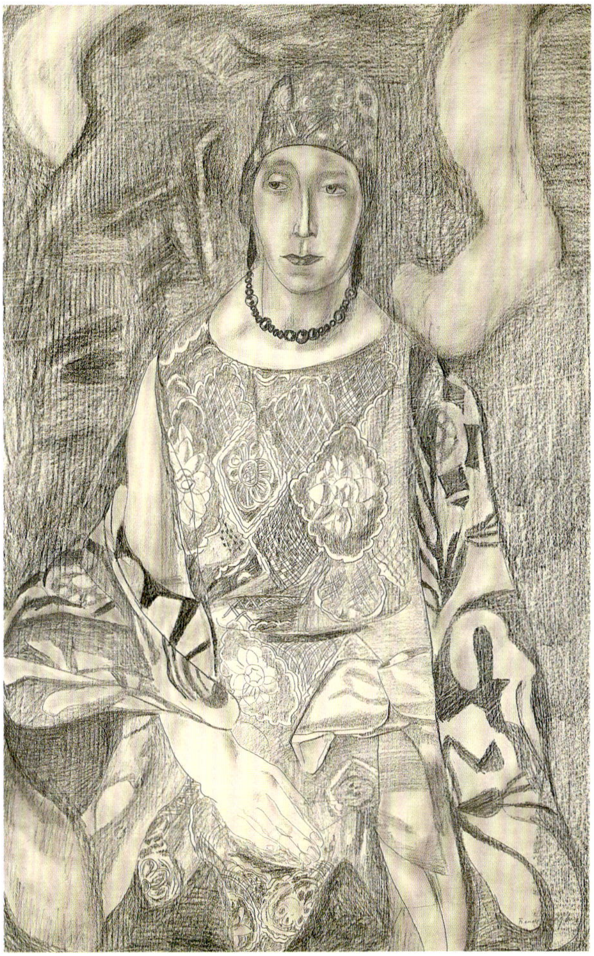

FRANCES HODGKINS
Seated Woman c 1925-30

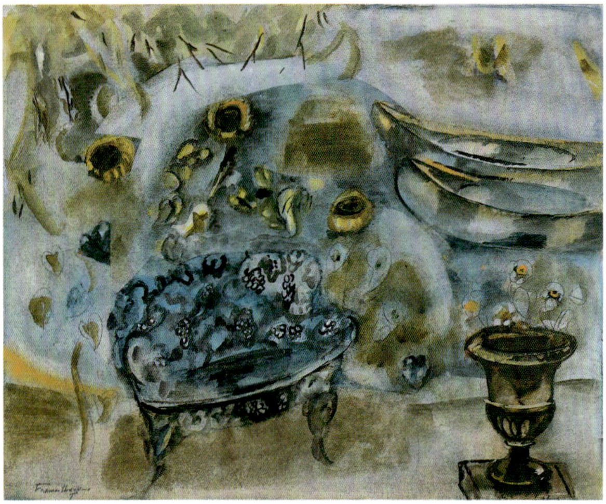

FRANCES HODGKINS
The Lake c 1930-35

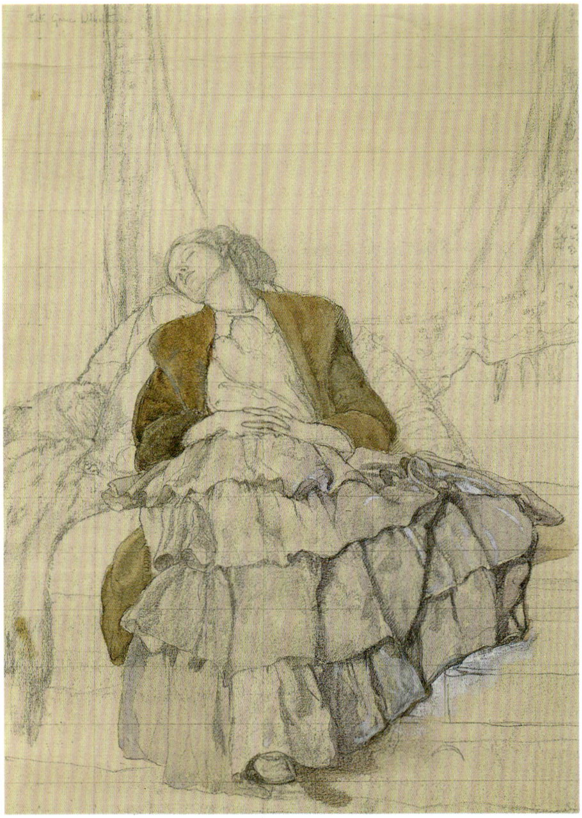

GRACE WHEATLEY
Seated Woman 1913

Aphrodite,
your garlands are made of golden leaves;

if only I
could have share in such good fortune

Sappho, 6th century BC[13]

if only I could share in such good fortune

Vanessa Bell's 'Studland Beach' c 1912, resonates the words 'if only' over and over again. In the foreground an adult woman and child sit on a sand dune. Their clothes are shades of red, their sunhats made of wicker. Between them and the group of five figures in the midground is a vast expanse of white sand. The background is a still sea of vivid blue. The distant figures are as one group. One figure, however, stands alone. 'if only'. Her long oatmeal coloured plait hangs heavily at the back of her neck. Her pale blue tunic and matching long skirt are solid blocks from which her undefined arms emerge stoically. At her feet four children play. Again one is alone. 'if only'. The other three play on, huddled together sharing secrets.

if only I could share in such good fortune

The ideas for 'The Lake' c 1930-35, by Frances Hodgkins, were probably stimulated by visits to the Severn, near Bridgnorth, with the artist Hannah Ritchie around 1930 and 1932. It is a delightful cacophony of sunflowers, boats, willow leaves, a couch and an incongruously solid urn with the lightest of flowers springing from its rim. Blues and browns are offset by touches of orange and yellow and the entire work, although unpeopled, has an aura of movement and gaiety about it that is quite in contrast to 'Studland Beach' with its illusion of freeze-frame.

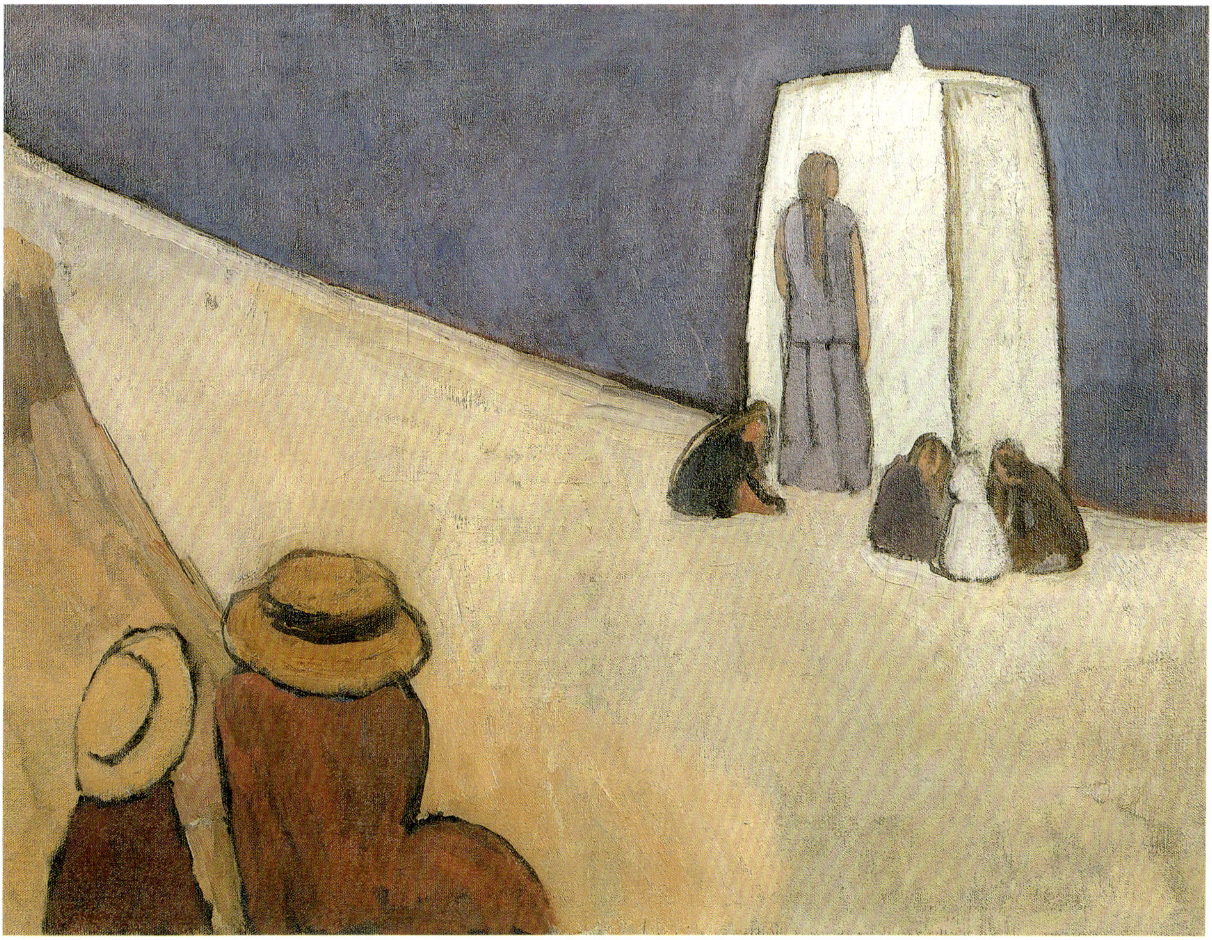

VANESSA BELL
Studland Beach c 1912

if only I could share in such good fortune

Edith Grace Wheatley's 'Seated Woman' 1913, is fully dressed in coat, skirt, blouse and shoes, asleep on a couch. Her fingers are tensely intertwined and her head falls heavily in deep repose. The artist has left visible the grid of lines which could later be used to enlarge the drawing, and she has signed the work. In this apparently unfinished work, the touches of watercolour which highlight the skirt and a firm block of colour delineating the fur of the coat seem strangely out of place. It is the only picture by Grace Wheatley in the Collection and offers little insight into the body of her work. It registers a presence which although acknowledged is neglected. In analysing the social and economic influences on painting women we touch upon factors which affect notions of femininity, women's role, and the construction of art histories.

It is a decade since the publication of *Old Mistresses: Women, Art and Ideology*. In their conclusion to that book Rozsika Parker and Griselda Pollock stated:

> Women's practice in art has never been absolutely forbidden, discouraged or refused, but rather contained and limited to its function as the means by which masculinity gains and sustains its supremacy in the important sphere of cultural production.
>
> The mapping out of a new framework and our revisions are relevant to both feminist historians and artists. We must understand the historical process and practices that have

> determined the current situation of women artists if we are to confront the role of cultural production and representations in the systems of sexual domination and power.[14]

This contestation remains true.

The white male Eurocentric nature of most of the works in the Tate Collection stands in stark contrast to the works by women artists. These are few in number and are even more randomly representative of their oeuvres than those of male artists. Such problems are exacerbated in the case of works by Black artists. In order for the Collection to be fully representative, works by women and Black artists must be increased by more than mere token gestures, and that must include the work of the greatest anachronism in European thought - the Blackwomanartist. Scholarship and analysis should be brought to bear on this noble task.

The paintings in *Echo: Works by Women Artists 1850-1940,* selected from the Tate Gallery Collection, are all, apparently, by white women and therefore articulate their own partial landscapes of desire. There were Blackwomen artists active in Europe during this period; painters and sculptors such as Edmonia Lewis based in Rome, Meta Vaux Warrick in Paris, Lois Mailou Jones also in Paris.

garlands made of golden leaves

Much of the impetus and vitality of Modernism was drawn from African art. For Black artists, this was an integral part of their cultural heritage and continuum. All artists draw from that which is around them, engage in dialogue through their work, and explore issues which appertain to them. The issue of identities and explorations of notions of femininity were central to Blackwomen's work during that period, just as they were to the women represented in *Echo.*

garlands made of golden leaves

For Blackwomen artists active today, there is a need to recognise continuity and parallels between practice then and now. As artists heading toward the twenty-first century we take, by any means necessary, ideas and inspiration to continue our struggle to contribute to global radical art practice. As Lubaina Himid stated in 'Mapping: A Decade of Black Women Artists 1980-1990':

> Being the first has its triumphs, keeping going is where the hard work begins. If we really believe we were the first black women to call ourselves artists we would have an excuse to give up, we were not, we are the continuum. We are part of an enormous international movement which stretches far back in time.[15]

garlands made of golden leaves

This poem by the contemporary Black British poet Bernardine Evaristo, is taken from a cycle of poems, in which Bernardine explores the politics of location.What it means for a Blackwoman of the African diaspora to travel.

SIMPLE SCRIBE

I am a simple scribe
looking out at the night Nile
surveying the lights
dabbling on the banks
where the Bedouins stay.

I am a simple scribe
capturing the colours of this land,
aligning my paper to learn the dimensions.

I am a simple scribe
remembering the trade of the people,
connecting the history
to our present lives.

I am a simple scribe
listening to the night life:
carriages and motors
rattle their way by.

I am a simple scribe
trying to learn so that I can pass on.
Trying to listen so that I can hear.
Trying to move so that I can enter[16].

As artists we journey in what appears to be an unchartered terrain. We are not alone. The Spirits of our ancestors travel with us. Ko Na Bra. The leaving and the return. A circle unbroken.

NOTES

1. Reprinted, *Imagist Poetry*, (ed. Peter Jones), London, 1972, p88.

2. *Taking Our Time* (ed. Freida Johles Forman with Caoran Sowton), London, 1989, p4.

3. Jill Morgan, 'Looking Into the Eyes of Flowers', *Ardentia Verba*, (ed. Lubaina Himid), Preston, l991, p16.

4. Toni Morrison, *Sula,* 1973, reprinted, London, 1982, p110.

5. *The Thin Black Line,* 1985, reprinted, Preston, 1990, p11.

6. Virginia Woolf, *Three Guineas,* London, 1938, p5.

7. Frances Spalding, *Vanessa Bell,* London, 1983, p108.

8. *ibid.*

9. *The Diary of Anne Frank,* Amsterdam, 1947, reprinted, London, 1954, p10.

10. Gertrude Stein, *Operas and Plays,* 1932, New York, 1987, p164.

11. Frances Steegmuller, *Apollinaire: Poet Among the Painters,* London, 1963, pp142-5.

12. Anne Allen Shockley, *Afro-American Women Writers 1746-1933,* New York, 1988, p378.

13. Fragment no.83, *Sappho: Poems and Fragments,* translated by Josephine Balmer, London, 1984, p82.

14. Griselda Pollock, and Rozsika Parker, *Old Mistresses: Women, Art and Ideology,* London, 1981, p170.

15. 'Mapping: A Decade of Black Women Artists 1980-1990', *Passion: Discourses on Blackwomens Creativity,* ed. Maud Sulter, Preston, 1990, p63.

16. Bernadine Evaristo, 'Thinking Around the Poems', ibid., p90.

ARTISTS' PROFILES & LIST OF WORKS

Dimensions: height followed by width in millimetres.

Identification numbers are those of the Tate Gallery catalogue.

Page numbers refer to illustrations of the works.

VANESSA BELL 1879-1961

Vanessa Stephen, elder sister of the writer Virginia Woolf, was both a painter and designer of pottery, textiles and interior decoration. She studied at the Royal Academy Schools, and briefly at the Slade. In 1907 she married Clive Bell, the art critic.

A member of the 'Bloomsbury Group', Vanessa Bell worked in the Omega Workshops under the direction of Roger Fry, and collaborated with Duncan Grant on many artistic projects. She founded the Friday Club in 1907, exhibited work in the Second Post-Impressionist Exhibition in 1912, *The New Movement in Art* show in 1917, and was a member of the London Group. She had her first solo show at the Independent Gallery in 1922.

She bore three children, Quentin, Angelica and Julian Bell. She died at Charleston, her home in Sussex, in 1961.

Studland Beach c 1912
Verso: *Group of Male Nudes*
by Duncan Grant c 1911
Oil on canvas
762 x 1016
Purchased 1976
T02080 (p25)

Abstract painting c 1914
Gouache on canvas
441 x 387
Purchased 1974
T01935 (p14)

Still Life on Corner of a Mantelpiece 1914
Oil on canvas
559 x 457
Purchased 1969
T01133 (p14)

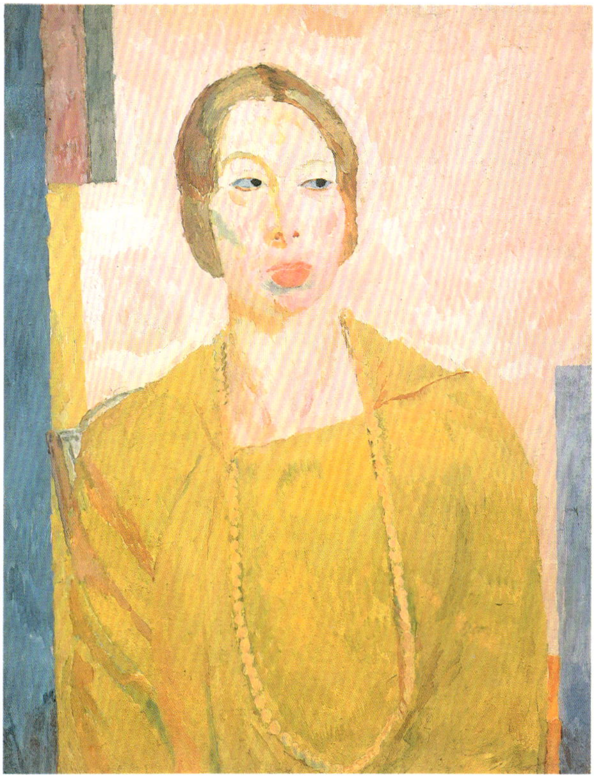

VANESSA BELL
Mrs St John Hutchinson 1915

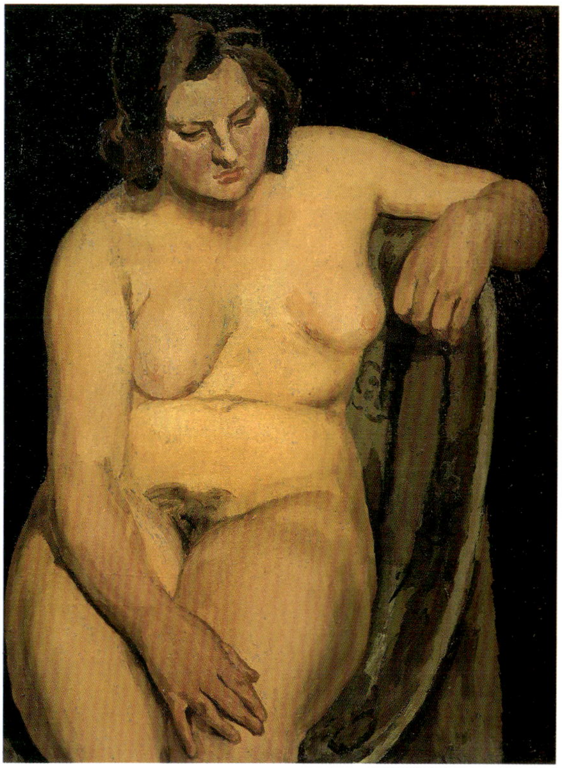

VANESSA BELL
Nude c 1922-23

Mrs St John Hutchinson 1915
Oil on board
737 x 578
Purchased 1973
T01768 (above)

Interior with a Table 1921
Oil on canvas
540 x 641
Bequeathed by Frank Hindley Smith 1940
N05078 (p17)

Nude c 1922-23
Oil on canvas
813 x 654
Bequeathed by Frank Hindley Smith 1940
N05077 (above)

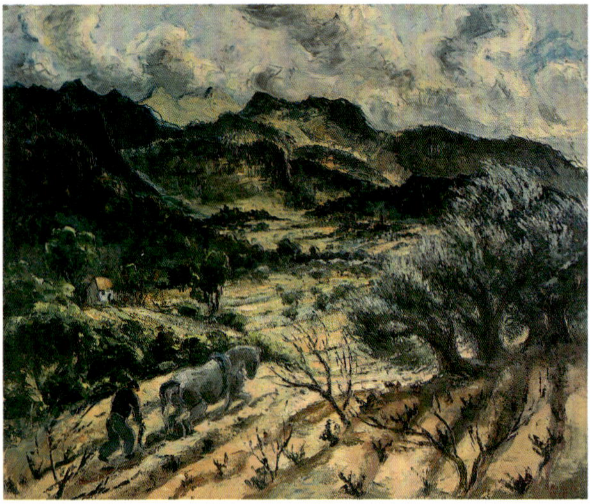

NADIA BENOIS
Near La Garde Freinet 1935

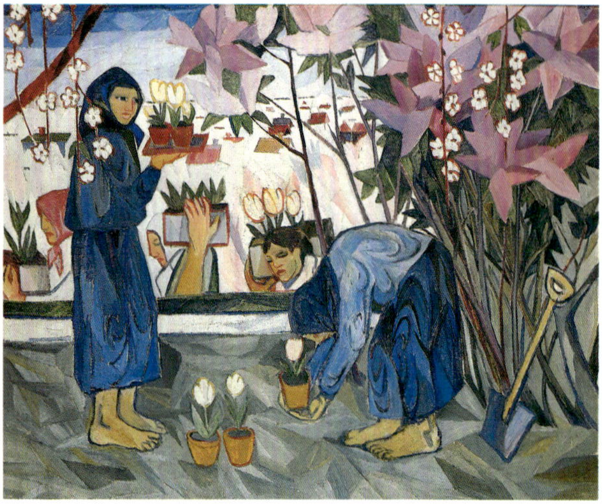

NATHALIE GONTCHAROVA
Gardening 1908

NADIA BENOIS 1896-1975

Nadia Benois was an author, stage designer and painter of still life and landscape works.

Born near St Petersburg in Russia into a family of artists and architects, she studied under Jacovleff, Choukhaieff and Alexandre Benois, her uncle.

In 1920 she married Jona Ustinov and in the same year left the Soviet Union to live in Britain. They had one son, the actor and dramatist Peter Ustinov. Her first solo show was at the Little Gallery in the Adelphi theatre in 1924. Nadia Benois exhibited with the New English Art Club from 1929 and was a member from 1937-41. In 1939 she designed the costumes and settings for *The Sleeping Princess* at Sadler's Wells.

Near La Garde Freinet 1935
Oil on canvas
635 x 762
Presented by the Contemporary Art Society 1936
N04855 (above)

FLORENCE ENGELBACH 1872-1951

Florence Neumegen was a painter of portraits, flowers and occasional landscapes. Born in Jerez de la Frontera in Spain of British parents she trained at Westminster School of Art, the Slade (c1894) and in Paris.

Her career seems to have been interrupted in 1902 when she married C R F Engelbach. After a period of many years she started painting again around 1930. Her first solo show was at the Beaux Arts Gallery in 1931.

Florence Engelbach exhibited at the Royal Academy from 1934-40, the Royal Institute of Oil Painters, and the Paris Salon. There was a memorial exhibition of her work at the Leicester Galleries in 1951.

Roses c1934-38
Oil on canvas
356 x 406
Presented anonymously 1939
N04978 (opposite)

NATHALIE GONTCHAROVA 1881-1962

Nathalie Gontcharova was born in Russia in 1881 at Nagaevo near Toula. Both a painter and designer, she trained at the School of Painting Sculpture and Architecture in Moscow from 1898-1902. She had intended to study sculpture but moved towards painting. Whilst a student, she met Michel Larionov who was also studying there. They lived as companions for the rest of her life.

In her one-woman show at the Art Salon in Moscow in 1913 she exhibited 761 works. She took part in a joint exhibition with Larionov in

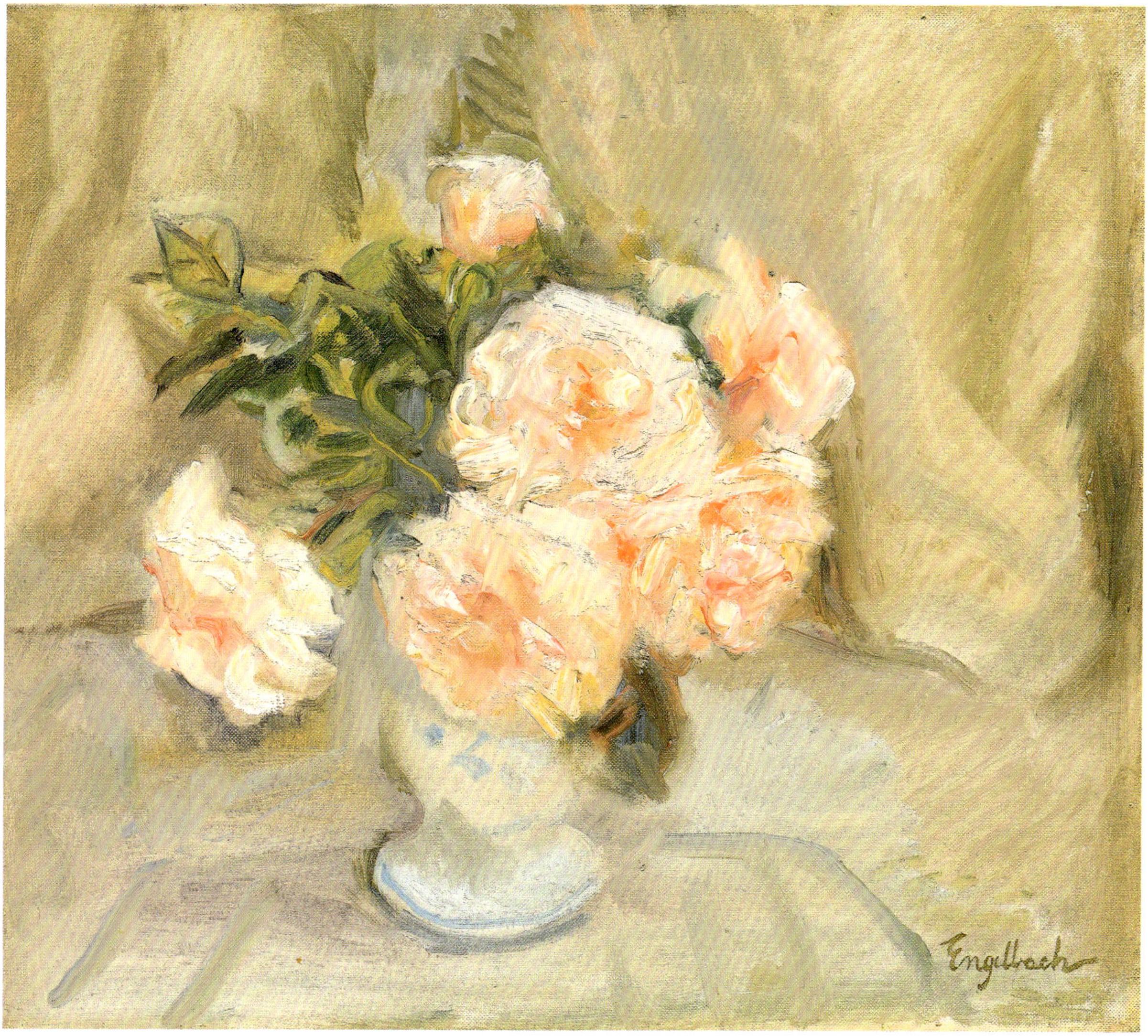

FLORENCE ENGELBACH
Roses c 1934-38

1914 in Paris and moved with him to Switzerland in 1914 to work with Diaghilev. Gontcharova designed sets and costume for several Diaghilev ballets including *Le Coq d'Or*, 1914 and *L'Oiseau de Feu,* 1926. Gontcharova settled in Paris in 1919 and continued to produce art periodically throughout her lifetime. She died in her adopted city in 1962.

Gardening 1908
Oil on canvas
1029 x 1232
Presented by the artist 1961
T00468 (opposite and back cover)

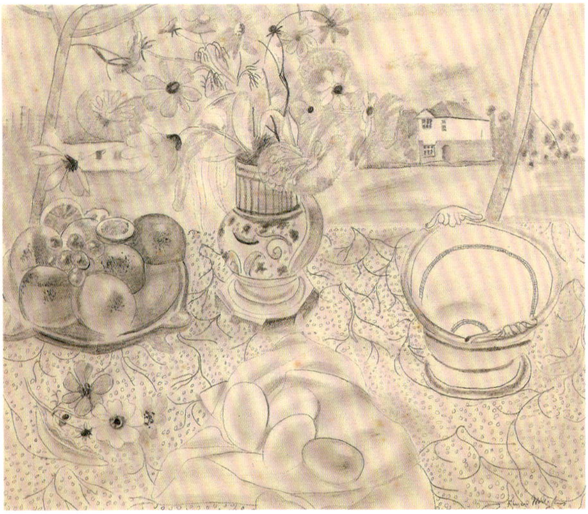

FRANCES HODGKINS
Still Life c 1929

FRANCES HODGKINS 1869-1947

Frances Hodgkins was born in Dunedin, Aotearoa (New Zealand) in 1869. A painter of portraits, landscapes and still lifes, she began exhibiting her works before she attended Dunedin Art School from 1895 to 1898. After her studies she worked as a teacher and illustrator before travelling to Europe in 1901.

Her first one-woman show was at the W B Paterson Gallery in London in 1907. In 1908 she settled in Paris and built a reputation as a watercolourist. Meanwhile she taught for one year at the Atelier Colarossi - the first woman to do so - and then established a school for watercolour painting of her own, also in Paris.

During visits to Aotearoa, 1904-6 and 1912-13, and to Australia 1912-13 she exhibited works she had created in Europe. Returning to England she spent the years 1914-19 mainly in Cornwall. Around this time she began to paint in oils.

A return to France in 1920 stimulated her development of a more modern style. Frances Hodgkins worked as a designer for Calico Printers in Manchester from 1925-27. A solo show at Claridge Gallery, London in 1928 announced the new style of her work. A member of the 7 + 5 Society, 1929-34, she spent her last years in England and died at Dorchester in 1947. The Commonwealth Institute Gallery held an exhibition of her work in 1969 to mark the centenary of her birth.

Loveday and Ann: Two Women with a Basket of Flowers 1915
Oil on canvas
673 x 673
Purchased 1944
N05456 (p19)

Seated Woman c 1925-30
Pencil and black crayon on paper
940 x 597
Purchased 1948
N05857 (p23)

Still Life c 1929
Pencil on paper
378 x 445
Presented by Miss Lilian Harmston in accordance with the wishes of Arthur Rowland Howell 1957
T00163 (opposite)

The Lake c 1930-35
Gouache on paper
432 x 546
Presented by the Contemporary Art Society 1940
N05130 (p24)

BEATRICE HOW 1867-1932

Beatrice How was born in Bideford, Devon in 1867. She studied at Herkomer's school at Bushey and at the Académie Delacluse in Paris from 1893.

Beatrice How lived most of her life in France and Holland making annual trips to Britain. During the 1914-18 war she stayed with her sister in a rectory in Yorkshire. During that period she painted many portraits of children and nurses. Like many women artists at the time she was active in war work, serving with the Red Cross.

Her oeuvre consisted mainly of women, children and flowers. She worked in and around Etaples, where she set up a studio, and other French coastal areas, as well as in Holland. Beatrice How exhibited regularly at the Paris Salon from 1902 and had several one woman shows in Parisian galleries. She was a full member of the Société nationale des Beaux-Arts.

Although her work was shown in Scotland and America and purchased for collections such as Glasgow City Art Gallery and Museums and the Victoria and Albert Museum, her work has remained little known in Britain.

She died while visiting a niece at Hoddesdon in Hertfordshire in 1932.

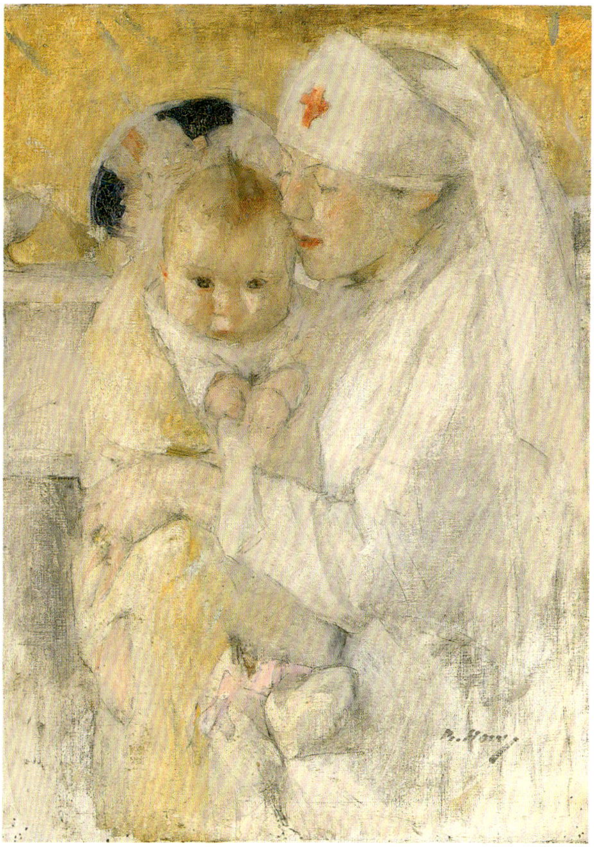

BEATRICE HOW
L'Infirmière c 1914-18

L'Infirmière c 1914-18
Oil on canvas
654 x 470
Presented by the Trustees of the Chantrey Bequest 1935
N04837 (above)

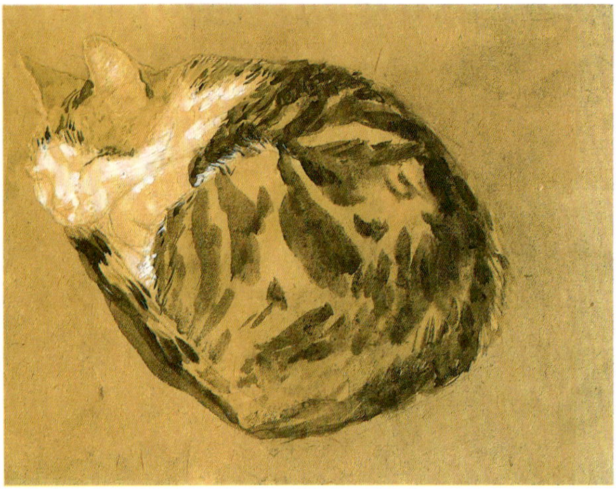

GWEN JOHN
Cat c 1904-8

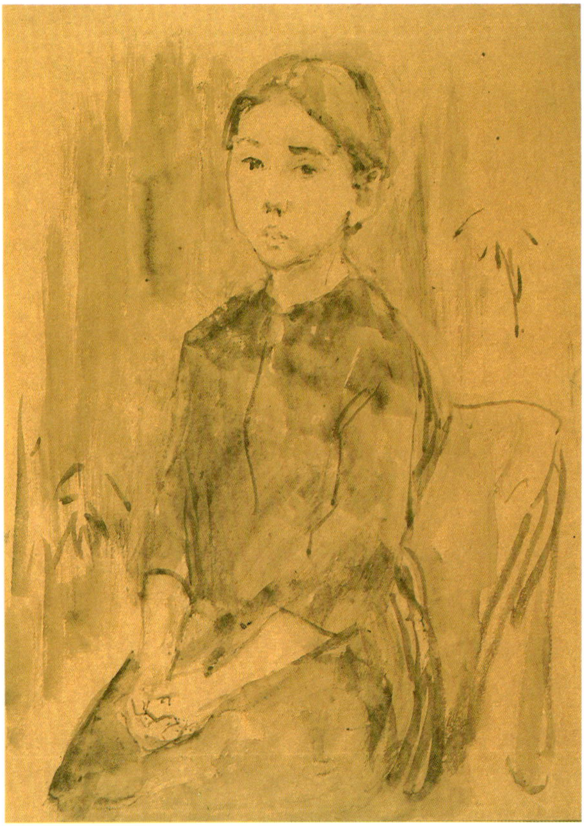

GWEN JOHN
Study of a Child c 1915-20

GWEN JOHN 1876-1939

Gwendoline John was born in Haverfordwest in Pembrokeshire in 1876. She studied at the Slade School 1894-97 and at the Académie Carmen in Paris for a year from 1898. She settled in France in 1903, making occasional visits to Britain but seldom exhibiting her work there. She did share an exhibition at the Carfax Gallery in 1903 with her younger brother Augustus. He prophesied, 'In fifty years from now I shall be known as the brother of Gwen John'.

She painted mainly portraits of women, girls and cats using women as both muse and model and was herself a model for many artists including members of the lesbian bohemia and Rodin's circle. In its picturing of women her work raises various questions about the representation of both 'woman' and the 'female gaze'. However one of her most well known works is an unpeopled interior 'A Corner of the Artist's Room' 1907-9, (Sheffield City Art Galleries) which contains several components of 'A Lady Reading'.

She died in Dieppe in September 1939. The Matthiesen Gallery staged a memorial exhibition of her work in 1946. Recent feminist scholarship, biographies and exhibitions of her work at Anthony d'Offay Gallery and the Barbican Art Gallery, have made Gwen John and her work more widely known in Britain.

Dorelia in a Black Dress c 1903-4
Oil on canvas
730 x 489
Presented by the Trustees of the Duveen Paintings Fund 1949
N05910 (p20)

Cat c 1904-8
Pencil and watercolour on paper
121 x 159
Presented by Miss Mary Constance Lloyd 1957
T00156 (above)

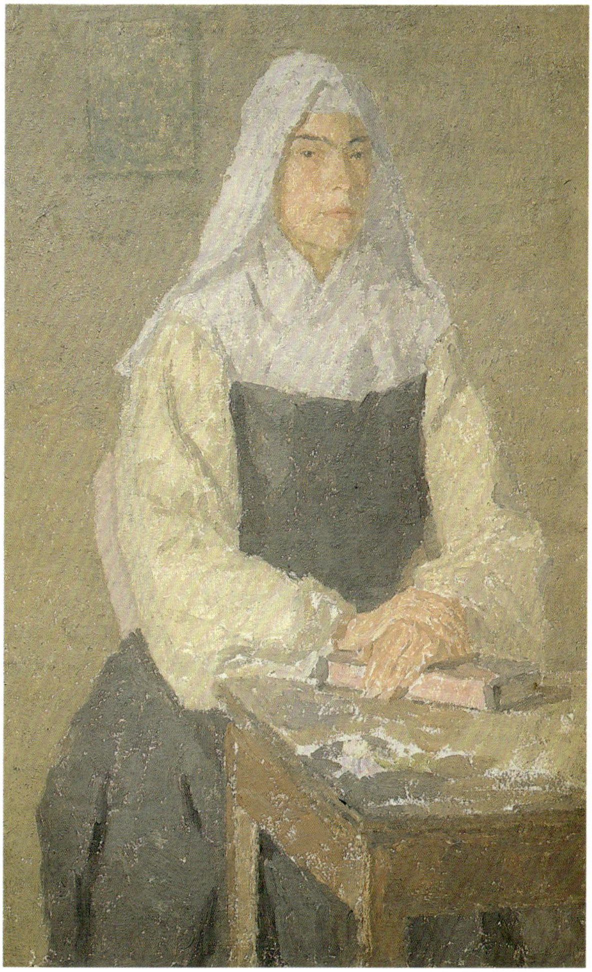

GWEN JOHN
The Nun c 1915-21

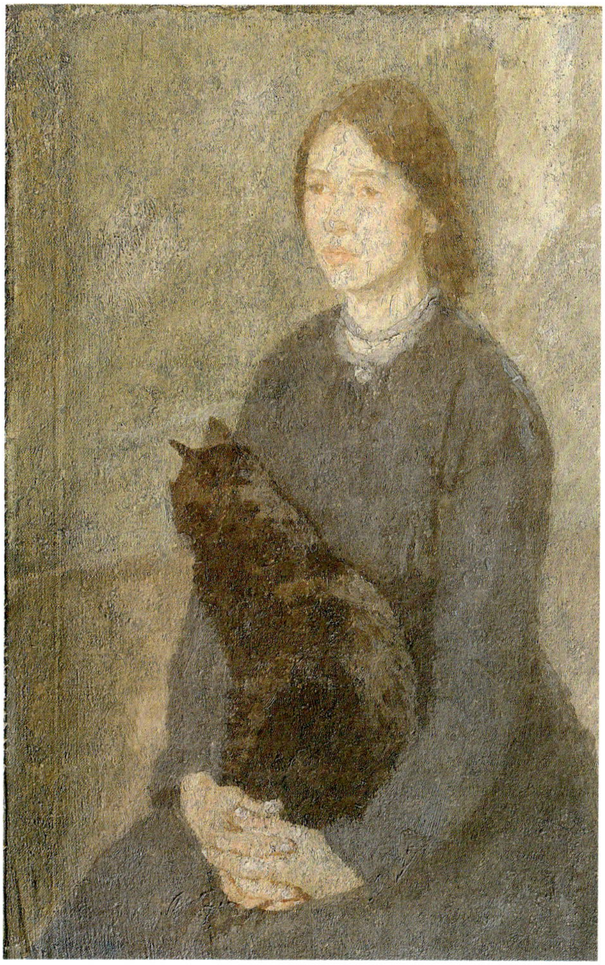

GWEN JOHN
Young Woman Holding a Black Cat
c 1920-25 (not in exhibition)

Nude Girl 1909-10
Oil on canvas
445 x 279
Presented by the Contemporary Art Society 1917
N03173 (p20)

A Lady Reading 1909-11
Oil on canvas
403 x 254
Presented by the Contemporary Art Society 1917
N03174 (p17)

Study of a Child c 1915-20
Watercolour on paper
324 x 251
Purchased 1940
N05152 (opposite)

The Nun c 1915-21
Oil on canvas
686 x 432
Purchased 1940
N05162 (above)

The Convalescent 1918-19
Oil on canvas
337 x 254
Bequeathed Mrs Rhoda Symons 1937
N04861 (p15)

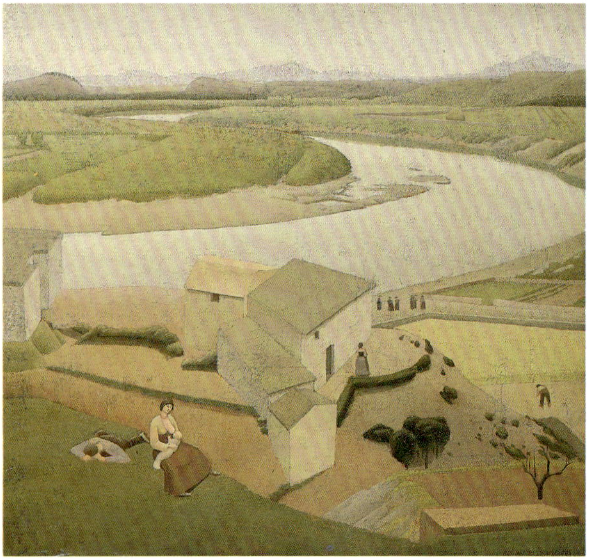

WINIFRED KNIGHTS
Italian Landscape 1921

WINIFRED KNIGHTS 1899-1947

Winifred Margaret Knights was born in London. She studied at the Slade School 1915-17 and 1918-20. Winner of a Slade Scholarship in 1919 and a Rome Scholarship in 1920, she worked in Rome from 1920-1925.

In 1924 she married Walter Thomas Monnington who was also an artist. Her work was exhibited at the Imperial Gallery 1927-31. Although she joined the New English Art Club in 1929 she never exhibited with it and resigned in 1931.

She died in London in 1947.

Italian Landscape 1921
Oil on natural wood panel
305 x 324
Purchased 1922
N03681 (above)

MARIE LAURENCIN 1885-1956

Marie Laurencin was born in Paris in 1885. She was not only a painter but also designer, illustrator and printmaker. She was an artist and poet and muse of Apollinaire, inspiring some of his finest poems. Their affair lasted from 1907 until 1913. They did not marry because of his mother's reservations about Marie's illegitimacy, which is ironic given that Apollinaire was also illegitimate.

Educated at the Lycée Lamartine, she then studied drawing at the Académie Humbert. Gertrude Stein was the first collector of Laurencin's work when she purchased 'Group of Artists', 1908. Her work was included in the first group show of Cubism at the Salon des Indépendants in 1911 and her first one woman show was in 1912 at the Galerie Barbazanges in Paris.

In 1914 she married Otto von Waetjen, an aristocratic German, and settled for the duration of the war in Barcelona. In 1920 the couple divorced and she returned to Paris.

Best known today for her pastel portraits of women, Marie Laurencin also carried out commissions for wallpaper and textile design, book illustration, set and costume designs for Diaghilev's *Ballet Russes* and dress designs for Paul Poiret.

Portraits 1915
Oil on canvas
330 x 460
Bequeathed by C Frank Stoop 1933
N04726 (p21)

GEORGIANA MACDONALD 1840-1920

Georgiana MacDonald, the fifth of eleven children, was born into a Methodist family in 1840.

She attended drawing classes at the School of Design in South Kensington, London and shared, with Emily Seddon, private classes with Ford Madox Brown where they painted from a model. These classes came to an end in 1858 when she took time out to care for a sick sister's child.

She was courted by Ned Jones (later Edward Burne-Jones, Baronet) from 1856 - she was fifteen and he twenty-two - until 1860 when they married. Her artistic career continued to be interrupted by motherhood, her husband's career, and the complicated web of the Pre-Raphaelite Group's affairs and intrigues. She did however carry out various craft projects with Jane Morris.

Later she became active in radical politics. In particular she campaigned to establish the South London Art Gallery in Southwark, making art accessible by having free admission. The Gallery is still committed to these principles, remains active today, and has recently celebrated its centenary.

An aunt of both Rudyard Kipling and Stanley Baldwin, Georgiana Burne-Jones moved in a circle of artists, writers and politicians. What would have become of her art had she prioritised her artistic skills over domestic concerns is however indeterminable.

Dead Bird 1857
Watercolour on paper
89 x 171
Presented by Mrs J W Mackail 1938
N04941 (above)

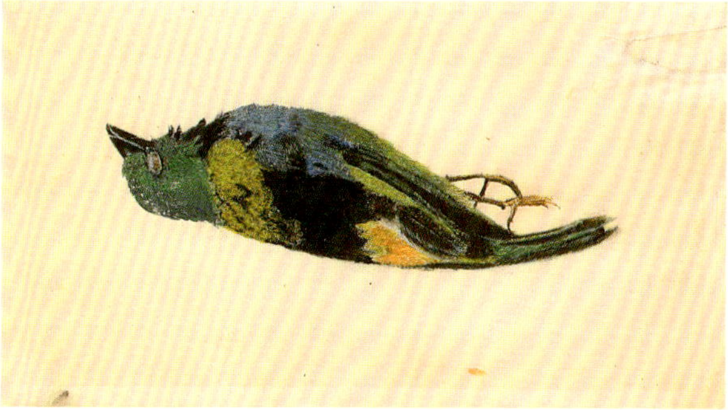

GEORGIANA MACDONALD
Dead Bird 1857

MARY McEVOY 1870-1941

Mary Edwards was born in Freshwood, Somerset in 1870.

A painter of portraits, interiors and flower paintings, her work demonstrates, in its sensitivity, a way of representing women and their concerns. In terms of physical space and female preoccupations, she gives voice to a language of psychological inner life while representing an everyday interior and pastime.

In 1902 she married Ambrose McEvoy, also an artist, and had a son, Michael. She exhibited extensively with the Fine Art Society, the Royal Academy, and at Knoedler's Gallery in London in 1933 and 1936.

Interior: Girl Reading 1901
Oil on canvas
533 x 438
Purchased 1927
N04362 (p22 and front cover)

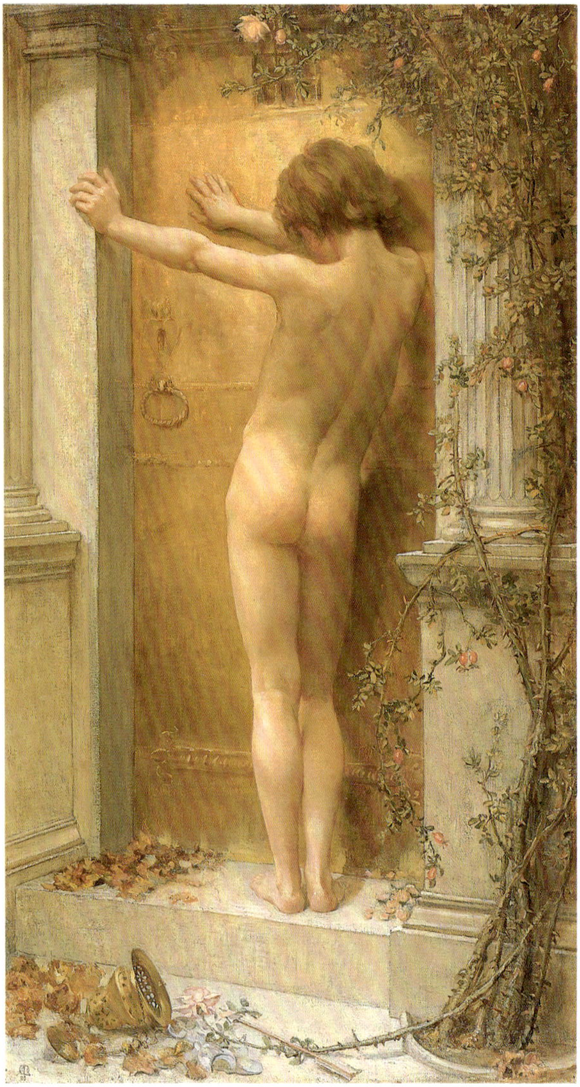

ANNA LEA MERRITT
Love Locked Out 1889

ANNA LEA MERRITT 1844-1930

Anna Lea was born in Philadelphia in 1844. She began studying drawing from the age of seven, and in 1867 made a European tour, which included Paris, Rome and Dresden. Her art studies continued during this period.

In London in 1871 she came under the influence of Henry Merritt, an artist and critic. Their relationship was strained and they did not marry until 1877, shortly before Merritt (who was considerably older than Anna Lea) died. He is, however, romantically glorified in her memoir of him, *Henry Merritt: Art Criticism and Romance,* written in 1879, which is illustrated with twenty-three of her own etchings.

Anna Lea Merritt's painting style is essentially classical, with sentimental, allegorical titles such as 'The Pied Piper of Hamelin' and 'Camilla'. Her paintings were exhibited at the Royal Academy for most of her career.

Although the artist settled permanently in Britain in 1890 she often visited America. She won accolades for two pictures at the Columbian Exposition, Chicago, in 1893, one for the painting 'Eve Overcome by Remorse', and one for a mural in the celebrated Woman's Building.

Love Locked Out c 1889
Oil on canvas
1156 x 641
Presented by the Trustees of the Chantrey Bequest 1890
N01578 (left)

BERTHE MORISOT 1841-1895

Berthe Morisot was born in Bourges in 1841 and moved to Paris with her upper middle class family in 1848. At an early age both she and her elder sister Edma studied art under various masters. Edma abandoned her artistic career when she married in 1869, whereas Berthe had the expediency to marry Eugène, younger brother of the painter Edouard Manet in 1874. Edouard's influence assured her the opportunity to continue her career.

Her contact with artists such as Corot, Daumier

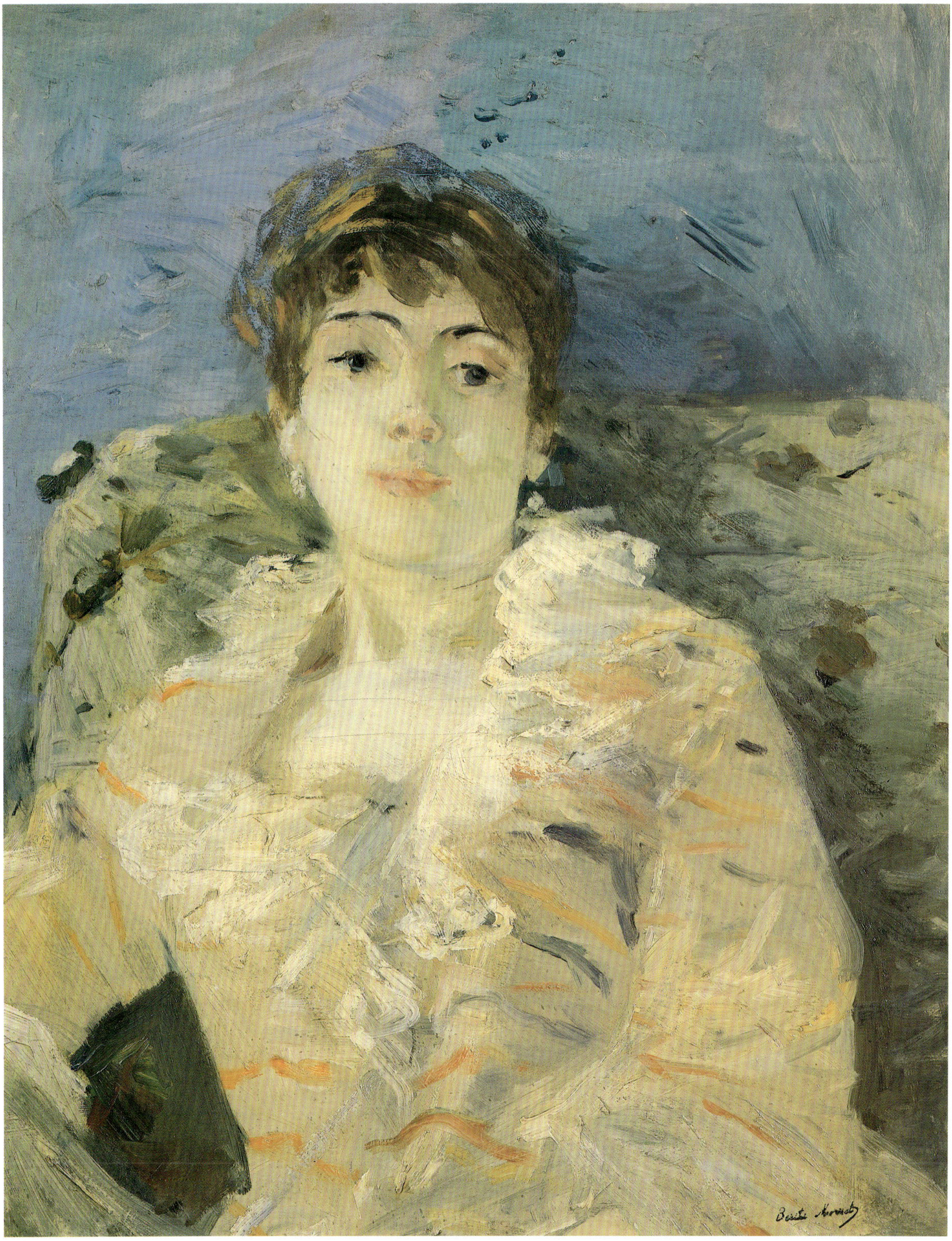

BERTHE MORISOT
Girl on a Divan c 1885

and Daubigny inspired her to work from nature. Berthe Morisot's successful *début* at the Paris Salon in 1864 was with two landscapes painted in 1863 at the river Oise; she continued to show at the Salon for the next decade.

Later as a member of the Impressionists she exhibited in all the group shows except in 1879 when she was pregnant. Her first one-woman show was in 1892. The centenary of her birth was celebrated with a retrospective at the Orangerie. As a woman artist, Berthe Morisot has been relatively well documented, sadly however not in the depth that, as a founder member of the modern movement, she deserves.

Girl on a Divan c1885
Oil on canvas
610 x 502
Bequeathed by the Hon Mrs A E Pleydell-Bouverie through the Friends of the Gallery 1968
T01079 (p39)

WINIFRED NICHOLSON 1893-1981

Winifred Roberts was born in Oxford in 1893. Her grandfather, the 9th Earl of Carlisle, was her first art teacher. She studied at Byam Shaw School of Art and later in Paris.

In 1920 she married Ben Nicholson, also an artist, and spent the winters of 1920-23 at Lake Lugano. Summers were spent in Cumberland. They exhibited together in London in 1923, and again in 1927 with Christopher Wood at the Beaux Arts Gallery. The Nicholsons were active members of the 7 + 5 Society until it ceased in 1935. The marriage broke up after eleven years, but friendship continued, with Winifred raising their three small children.

She spent time in Paris from 1932-38 and began a period of abstract painting. She exhibited these works under the name of Winifred Dacre. In an article in *Circle: an International Survey of Constructive Art*, edited by Ben Nicholson and Naum Gabo, and published in 1937, she declared that:

> It is no longer necessary to set about seeking some form into which the colour may be tagged to give it meaning.

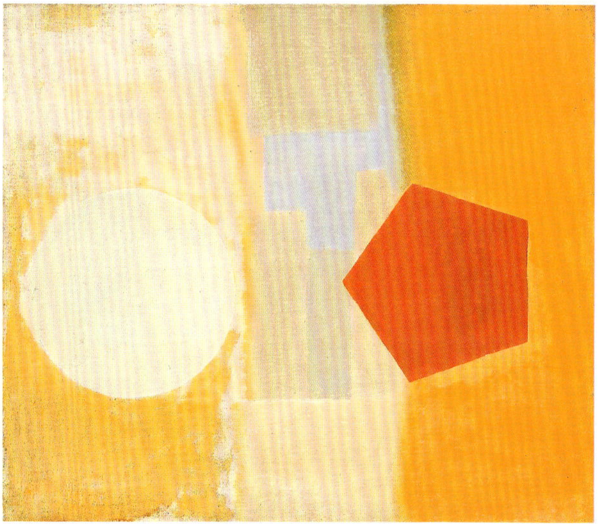

WINIFRED NICHOLSON
Moonlight and Lamplight 1937

In the following year she was instrumental in bringing Mondrian from Paris to London. On her return to her home in Cumberland she once again painted landscapes and still lifes. She continued to travel and paint all her life.

Her work was exhibited frequently in London, and the Third Eye Gallery, Glasgow staged a retrospective of her work in 1979, which toured throughout Scotland and England. It was a validation, within her lifetime, of her career as an artist.

Winifred Nicholson died at her home in Cumbria in 1981. The Tate Gallery held a retrospective exhibition in 1987.

Window-Sill, Lugano 1923
Oil on board
286 x 508
Presented by the Contemporary Art Society 1940
N05126 (p16)

Moonlight and Lamplight 1937
Oil on canvas
762 x 889
Purchased 1975
T01996 (above)

DOD PROCTOR 1891-1972

Dod (Doris) Shaw lived in Newlyn from girlhood and studied art under the supervision of Stanhope and Elizabeth Forbes from 1907-08 and for a short time at the Atelier Colarossi in Paris. Dod Shaw met Laura Knight when the Knights moved to Newlyn in 1908. In 1912 Dod married Ernest Proctor, also an artist. The following year she gave birth to a son.

Dod Proctor first exhibited at the Royal Academy in 1916 and continued to do so frequently throughout her life. In 1934 she became the third female Associate member of the Royal Academy and in 1942 was only the second woman to gain full membership this century, following in the footsteps of Laura Knight who had been elected RA in 1936.

When her work 'Morning' was exhibited at the Royal Academy Summer Exhibition in 1927 it caused a sensation. This picture, of a young woman captured by the viewer asleep in the morning sun, caught the nation's attention thanks to publicity stirred up by the *Daily Mail* newspaper, which purchased the work. It toured to 23 provincial galleries during 1927-29 and travelled on to America. On both Atlantic crossings the work was displayed on board ship. The work was then given to the Tate by the newspaper as a gift to the nation.

When Ernest died in 1935 Dod gave up the London studio and returned to Newlyn. She often travelled abroad with the artist Althea Garstin and found new artistic inspiration in the exotic.

Kitchen at Myrtle Cottage c1930-35
Oil on canvas
641 x 762
Presented by the Trustees of the Chantrey Bequest 1935
N04817 (p16)

The Orchard c1934
Oil on canvas
1016 x 1270
Presented by the Trustees of the Chantrey Bequest 1937
N05325 (above)

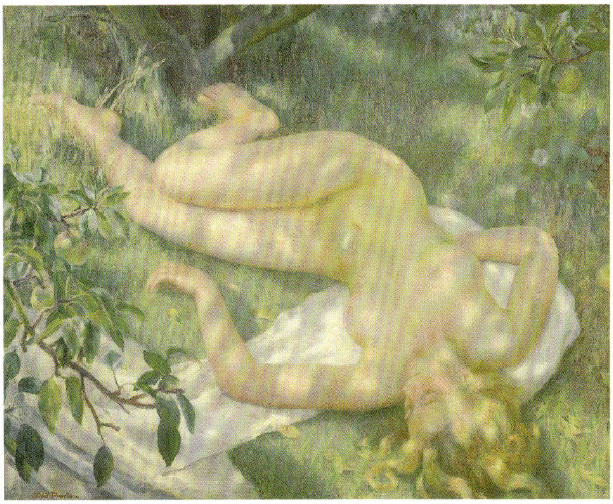

DOD PROCTOR
The Orchard c1934

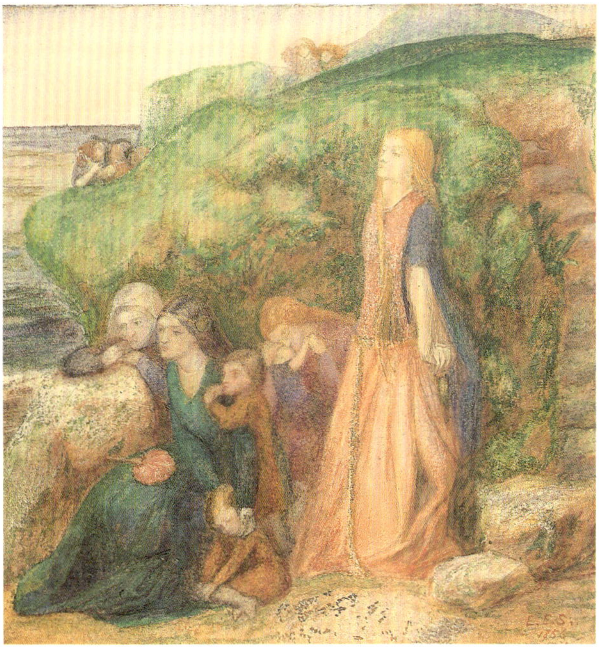

ELIZABETH ELEANOR SIDDAL
Sir Patrick Spens 1856

ELIZABETH ELEANOR SIDDAL 1829-1862

Elizabeth Eleanor Siddall was born in London on 25 July 1829, one of eight children. Her mother was a Cockney, and her father an ironmonger from Sheffield.

Trained as a milliner she supplemented her wages by modelling for artists from early 1850. By 1852 she had determined to be an artist. Her poetry also developed in works such as *Gone:*

GONE

To touch the glove upon her tender hand,
To watch the jewel sparkle in her ring,
Lifted my heart into a sudden song
As when the wild birds sing.

To touch her shadow on the sunny grass,
To break her pathway through the darkened
wood,
Filled all my life with trembling and tears
And silence where I stood.

I watch the shadows gather round my heart,
I live to know that she is gone -
Gone Gone for ever, like the tender dove
That left the Ark alone.

Poems and Drawings of Elizabeth Siddall,
ed. R C Lewis and M S Lasner, 1978, p12

Loss is a recurring theme in the artist's work. In 'Sir Patrick Spens' we see a group of women and children looking out to sea waiting for sailors who will never return. The theme is taken from a traditional ballad;

O lang may thy ladies sit
With fans in their hands
Waitin tae see Sir Patrick Spens
Come sailin in tae land.

Elizabeth Siddall married Gabriel Dante Rossetti in May 1860, suffered the stillborn birth of a daughter in April 1861 and died in February 1862 aged 32, of an overdose of laudanum. She is buried in Highgate cemetery in the Rossetti family plot.

Unlike almost all of the women in this exhibition Elizabeth Eleanor Rossetti was a member of the working class. This meant that she had no access to the genteel pursuits thought suitable for middle class women of the period. Painting and drawing were seen as feminine accomplishments which helped 'finish' a girl's education. Although most artists in *Echo* went on to create some sort of artistic career it was auto-didactism which motivated Elizabeth to pursue the identity of artist and poet.

Sir Patrick Spens 1856
Watercolour on paper
241 x 229
Purchased 1919
N03471 (above)

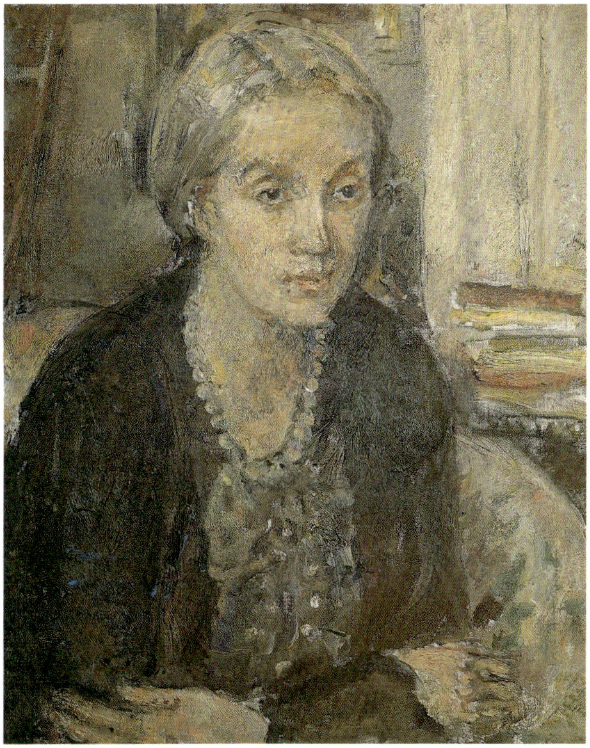

DAME ETHEL WALKER
Vanessa 1937

DAME ETHEL WALKER 1861-1951

Ethel Walker was born in Edinburgh in 1861. She studied at Westminster and the Slade art schools. She spent most of her adult life living in London in her Cheyne Walk studio or spending time at a cottage in Robin Hood's Bay Yorkshire, accompanied always by her wire fox terrier companions.

Ethel Walker painted mainly portraits, seascapes, flower pieces and murals. Her interest in picturing women is well illustrated in pictures such as 'The Spanish Gesture' (Walker Art Gallery, Liverpool) purchased 1937, 'The Artist's Stepmother' c1899, and 'Self-Portrait' ?exh 1930, both in the Tate Collection. The latter work was painted in just two and a half hours when the artist was aged over sixty. Another work, 'Nausicaa', which was also bought by the Tate Gallery, represented British Art at the 1939 World Trade Fair in Chicago.

She was a member of the New English Art Club from 1900. Although she exhibited regularly at the Royal Academy, she was not elected an Associate member until 1940. She was made a Dame of the British Empire in 1943.

A memorial exhibition of her work was held at the Tate Gallery in 1951 as part of a show of three women artists, featuring Dame Ethel, Gwen John and Frances Hodgkins.

Vanessa 1937
Oil on canvas
610 x 508
Presented by the Contemporary Art Society 1939
N05038 (left)

GRACE WHEATLEY 1881-1970

Edith Grace Wolfe was born in London in 1881. A painter and watercolourist, she trained at the Slade and in Paris. Time spent in Newquay, Cornwall, in 1913, suggests that she was working alongside or knew of other women artists such as Gluck, Laura Knight, Dod Proctor and Althea Garstin.

Prior to her appointment as Senior Lecturer in Fine Art at the University of Cape Town, Azania (South Africa), she married John Wheatley who was Professor of Fine Art at the same institution. She held her post from 1925 until 1937, when her husband was appointed Director of Sheffield Art Galleries.

Grace Wheatley exhibited her work at the New English Art Club, Royal Academy and Royal Society of British Artists. Her work is also in the collection of the British Museum and Sheffield City Art Galleries. Her obituary in *The Times* on 2 December 1970 records that she had one daughter.

Seated Woman 1913
Pencil, watercolour and gouache on paper
356 x 254
Purchased 1922
N03642 (p24)

SELECT BIBLIOGRAPHY & FURTHER READING

Barbican Art Gallery, *The Edwardian Era*, London, 1987

Baron, Wendy, *Miss Ethel Sands and Her Circle*, London, 1977

Feminist Art News Various issues including:

Passion: Blackwomens Creativity of the African Diaspora, ed. Lubaina Himid and Maud Sulter, FAN, Leeds, 1988

150 Years of Photography, ed. Jane Beckett and Maud Sulter, FAN, Leeds, 1989

Women, Modernism and Modernity, ed. Deborah Cherry, Jane Beckett, Lubaina Himid & Maud Sulter, FAN, Leeds, 1990

Forman, Freida Johles, with Sowton, Caoron, ed., *Taking Our Time: Feminist Perspectives on Temporality*, London, 1989

Frank, Anne, *The Diary of Anne Frank*, Amsterdam, 1947

Harris, Anne Sutherland and Nochlin, Linda, *Women Artists 1550-1950*, New York, 1984

Heresies Various issues including:

Racism Is The Issue, vol.4, no.3, New York, 1984

Himid, Lubaina, ed., *Ardentia Verba*, Preston, 1991

Howe, Marie Jenney, ed. and translated, *George Sand: The Intimate Journal*, Chicago, 1977

Institute of Contemporary Art, *The Thin Black Line*, London, 1985, reprinted by Urban Fox Press, ed. Lubaina Himid, Preston, 1990

Jeffreys, Sheila, *The Spinster And Her Enemies: Feminism and Sexuality* 1880-1930, London, 1985

Jones, Peter ed., *Imagist Poetry*, London, 1972

Morrison, Toni, *Sula*, London, 1982

Museum of Modern Art, *Four Americans in Paris: The Collections of Gertrude Stein and Her Family*, New York, 1970

Nunn, Pamela Gerrish, *Victorian Women Artists*, London, 1987

Petersen, Karen, and Wilson, J J, *Women Artists: Recognition and Reappraisal from the Early Middle Ages to the Twentieth Century*, London, 1978

Pollock, Griselda, and Parker, Rozsika, *Old Mistresses: Women, Art and Ideology*, London, 1981

Rochdale Art Gallery, *Painting Women*, Rochdale, 1987

Rubenstein, Charlotte Streifer, *American Women Artists: From Early Indian Times to The Present*, New York, 1982

Shockley, Ann Allen, *Afro-American Women Writers 1746-1933: An Anthology and Critical Guide*, New York, 1988

Spalding, Frances, *Vanessa Bell*, London, 1983

Stein, Gertrude, *The Autobiography of Alice B Toklas*, London, 1966

Stein, Gertrude, *Operas and Plays*, Chicago, 1987

Sterling, Dorothy, ed., *We Are Your Sisters: Black Women in the Nineteenth Century*, New York, 1984

Sulter, Maud, *Zabat: Narratives*, Preston, 1989

Sulter, Maud, ed., *Passion: Discourses On Blackwomens Creativity*, Preston, 1990

Sulter, Maud, *Hysteria*, Preston, 1991

Walker Art Gallery, *Women's Works*, Liverpool, 1988

Woolf, Virginia, *A Room of One's Own*, London, 1929

Woolf, Virginia, *Three Guineas*, London, 1938